Distribution and Movement of Bull Trout in the Upper Jarbidge River Watershed, Nevada

By M. Brady Allen, Patrick J. Connolly, Matthew G. Mesa, Jodi Charrier, and Chris Dixon

Prepared in cooperation with the U.S. Fish and Wildlife Service

Open-File Report 2010–1033

U.S. Department of the Interior
U.S. Geological Survey

U.S. Department of the Interior
KEN SALAZAR, Secretary

U.S. Geological Survey
Marcia K. McNutt, Director

U.S. Geological Survey, Reston, Virginia: 2010

For more information on the USGS—the Federal source for science about the Earth, its natural and living resources, natural hazards, and the environment, visit *http://www.usgs.gov* or call 1-888-ASK-USGS.

For an overview of USGS information products, including maps, imagery, and publications, visit *http://www.usgs.gov/pubprod*

To order this and other USGS information products, visit *http://store.usgs.gov*

Suggested citation:
Allen, M.B., Connolly, P.J., Mesa, M.G., Charrier, Jodi, and Dixon, Chris, 2010, Distribution and movement of bull trout in the upper Jarbidge River watershed, Nevada: U.S. Geological Survey Open-File Report 2010-1033, 80 p.

Contents

Figures

Tables

Conversion Factors and Datums

Conversion Factors

Multiply	By	To obtain
centimeter (cm)	0.3937	inch (in.)
millimeter (mm)	0.03937	inch (in.)
meter (m)	3.281	foot (ft)
kilometer (km)	0.6214	mile (mi)
square kilometer (km^2)	0.3861	square mile (mi^2)
gram (g)	0.03527	ounce, avoirdupois (oz)

Temperature in degrees Celsius (°C) may be converted to degrees Fahrenheit (°F) as follows:
°F=(1.8×°C)+32
Temperature in degrees Fahrenheit (°F) may be converted to degrees Celsius (°C) as follows:
°C=(°F-32)/1.8

Datums

Horizontal coordinate information is referenced to the World Geodetic System of 1984 (WGS84) datum.
Vertical coordinate information is referenced to the WGS84 EGM96 geoid.
Altitude, as used in this report, refers to distance above the vertical datum.

Distribution and Movement of Bull Trout in the Upper Jarbidge River Watershed, Nevada

By M. Brady Allen, Patrick J. Connolly, Matthew G. Mesa, Jodi Charrier, and Chris Dixon

Abstract

In 2006 and 2007, we surveyed the occurrence of bull trout (*Salvelinus confluentus*), the relative distributions of bull trout and redband trout (*Oncorhynchus mykiss*), and stream habitat conditions in the East and West Forks of the Jarbidge River in northeastern Nevada and southern Idaho. We installed passive integrated transponder (PIT) tag interrogation systems at strategic locations within the watershed, and PIT-tagged bull trout were monitored to evaluate individual fish growth, movement, and the connectivity of bull trout between streams. Robust bull trout populations were found in the upper portions of the East Fork Jarbidge River, the West Fork Jarbidge River, and in the Pine, Jack, Dave, and Fall Creeks. Small numbers of bull trout also were found in Slide and Cougar Creeks. Bull trout were numerically dominant in the upper portions of the East Fork Jarbidge River, and in Fall, Dave, Jack, and Pine Creeks, whereas redband trout were numerically dominant throughout the rest of the watershed. The relative abundance of bull trout was notably higher at altitudes above 2,100 m.

This study was successful in documenting bull trout population connectivity within the West Fork Jarbidge River, particularly between West Fork Jarbidge River and Pine Creek. Downstream movement of bull trout to the confluence of the East Fork and West Fork Jarbidge River both from Jack Creek (rkm 16.6) in the West Fork Jarbidge River and from Dave Creek (rkm 7.5) in the East Fork Jarbidge River was detected. Although bull trout exhibited some downstream movement during the spring and summer, much of their emigration occurred in the autumn, concurrent with decreasing water temperatures and slightly increasing flows. The bull trout that emigrated were mostly age-2 or older, but some age-1 fish also emigrated. Upstream movement by bull trout was detected less than downstream movement. The overall mean annual growth rate of bull trout in the East Fork and West Fork Jarbidge River was 36 mm. This growth rate is within the range reported in other river systems and is indicative of good habitat conditions. Mark-recapture methods were used to estimate a population of 147 age-1 or older bull trout in the reach of Jack Creek upstream of Jenny Creek.

Introduction

The Jarbidge River population of bull trout (*Salvelinus confluentus*) was listed as threatened under the Endangered Species Act on April 8, 1999 (64 Federal Register 17110). Bull trout within the Jarbidge River are presumably limited to a single core area within the upper watershed, which comprises six local populations: (1) East Fork Jarbidge River (including the East Fork headwaters, Cougar Creek, and Fall Creek); (2) West Fork Jarbidge River (including Sawmill Creek); (3) Dave Creek; (4) Jack Creek; (5) Pine Creek; and (6) Slide Creek (U.S. Fish and Wildlife Service, 2004). Bull trout populations in these areas are thought to be mostly local, with few migratory (fluvial) fish present. In 2004, the Jarbidge River Bull Trout Recovery Team estimated that fewer than 500 bull trout, with 50–125 reproductively mature fish, were present within the core area (U.S. Fish and Wildlife Service, 2004). Several factors are suspected to have limited the Jarbidge River bull trout population historically, including livestock grazing, elevated water temperatures, road construction and maintenance, mining, and hatchery supplementation of rainbow trout (*Oncorhynchus mykiss*) (U.S. Fish and Wildlife Service, 2004). Stocking of hatchery rainbow trout was suspended in 1998.

In 2006, the U.S. Fish and Wildlife Service (USFWS) formed a cooperative agreement with the U.S. Geological Survey's (USGS) Columbia River Research Laboratory (CRRL) for USGS to collect information on the life history, movements, abundance, and distribution of bull trout in the upper Jarbidge River basin. This information was needed to assist managers in making informed decisions regarding bull trout recovery. The objectives of the resulting study were to: (1) monitor the movements, distribution, and growth of bull trout in selected tributaries of the Jarbidge River basin; (2) estimate the abundance of selected local bull trout populations; (3) conduct habitat surveys and assess habitat conditions; and (4) use the data collected as a baseline to develop a cost-effective monitoring strategy to assess population trends over time until recovery is achieved. The USGS investigators regularly coordinated with the Jarbidge River Bull Trout Recovery Team, which comprises staff members from the Idaho Department of Environmental Quality, Bureau of Land Management (BLM), Nevada Department of Wildlife (NDOW), the U.S. Forest Service (USFS), USFWS, and Idaho Department of Fish and Game. This report summarizes study findings from 2006 and 2007.

Description of Study Site

The headwaters of the Jarbidge River are in the Jarbidge Mountains of northeastern Nevada. The watershed is characterized by an elevated volcanic plateau that gradually slopes northward to the Snake River Plain, which drains approximately 1,264 km^2 (488 mi^2; U.S. Fish and Wildlife Service, 2004). The upper watershed has a mountainous north-south crest with eight peaks greater than 3,050 m (10,000 ft) high. The East Fork and West Fork of the Jarbidge River flow northward for about 36 and 32 km, respectively, and merge about 6.4 km downstream of the Idaho-Nevada border. This confluence of the two forks was the downstream extent of our study area (fig. 1). The mainstem Jarbidge River continues another 45 km northwest and eventually empties into the Bruneau River in Idaho. Riparian vegetation in the watershed consists of juniper (*Juniperus spp.*), black cottonwood (*Populus balsamifera*), subalpine fir (*Abies lasiocarpa*), aspen (*Populus tremuloides*), and various forbs, grasses, and sedges (U.S. Fish and Wildlife Service, 2004). The Jarbidge Mountains have a subalpine climate and receive substantial amounts of precipitation, primarily in the form of snow, which is the major source of water for streams in the basin. Additional precipitation falls as rain during thunderstorms. Runoff follows the natural hydrograph, with high spring and early summer flows that diminish in the late summer but increase slightly during fall and winter. The only streamgaging station in the watershed is within our study area on the West Fork Jarbidge River downstream of Jarbidge, Nevada (USGS station number 13162225).

Study Methods

Fish Collection and Tagging

We sampled all streams within the Jarbidge River basin known to contain bull trout as identified by the Jarbidge River Bull Trout Recovery Team. These included parts of the East Fork and West Fork Jarbidge River, and Cougar, Fall, Slide, Dave, Jack, and Pine Creeks (figs. 2 and 3; tables 1, 2, and 3). In an attempt to find other streams containing bull trout, we conducted exploratory sampling in selected reaches of Deer, Buck, Sawmill, and God's Pocket Creeks, and on an unnamed tributary of the East Fork Jarbidge River. Successive samples were collected in an upstream direction with the goal of reaching the end of fish distribution while tagging as many bull trout as possible of the appropriate size. In several streams, some sections were skipped in an effort to sample reaches with higher bull trout densities, which maximized the returns of the effort given the time allotted. The upper end of fish distribution was confirmed by electrofishing upstream of the likely barrier for approximately 100 m where practicable.

Bull trout samples were collected using a Smith-Root model 15-B backpack electrofisher equipped with one small probe and one "rat tail" electrode. Each stream reach was electrofished in a single upstream pass and all habitats likely to contain bull trout were sampled. All observed bull trout were captured. Redband trout were not captured, but were enumerated and generally classified as being less than 80 mm, 80 to 150 mm, or larger than 150 mm in pools only. The occurrence of redband trout in pools was recorded to indicate their general abundance without overly slowing the progress of the sampling crew that would have resulted if redband trout had been counted and classified in the much longer non-pool sections as well. The general abundance of other fish species was noted as rare, present, or highly abundant. All captured bull trout were anesthetized with a 50-mg/L solution of tricaine methanesulfonate (MS-222), measured fork length to the nearest millimeter, weighed to the nearest 0.1 g, and inspected for reproductive status and external signs of disease or injury.

We tagged bull trout using full-duplex SGL model passive integrated transponder (PIT) tags (manufactured by Biomark, Inc., Boise, Idaho) that were 12 mm in length and operated at a frequency of 134.2 kHz. Fish less than 70 mm were considered too small to tag. In fish between 70 and 120 mm long, tags were injected into the peritoneal cavity. Fish greater than 120 mm were tagged in the dorsal sinus to minimize the potential for shedding of tags during spawning. A sample of caudal fin tissue was removed from most bull trout, placed in a pre-labeled vial containing 2 mL of 100% non-denatured ethanol, and sent to the USFWS's Abernathy Fish Technology Center (Longview, Wash.) for genetic analysis as part of a separate, but coordinated study (De Haan and others, 2007). Where bull trout were locally abundant, a genetic sample was taken from a subset of bull trout; otherwise a genetic sample was collected from each fish. After they recovered from the effects of tagging, fish were released in the location of capture.

In 2007, we conducted a Petersen mark-recapture population estimate for bull trout in Jack Creek. To facilitate repeatability, Jack Creek was selected because of ease of access and the known presence of a bull trout population. The population was estimated in two sections of Jack Creek: from the confluence with West Fork Jarbidge River upstream to the confluence of Jenny Creek (rkm 1.8); and upstream of Jenny Creek to the end of fish distribution (rkm 5.4). Three block nets and a picket weir were placed consecutively at the downstream end of each section to ensure a closed population. We electrofished the sections in one slow, methodical upstream pass, each within 1 day. In both the 3.6 km section upstream of Jenny Creek and the 1.8 km section downstream, three people started at the block nets on the downstream end, and three others started at the mid point. Only bull trout longer than 80 mm (age-1 or older) were included in the estimate. We tagged all captured bull trout, and the recapture effort occurred 24-30 h later.

Habitat Sampling

Along with electrofishing, we conducted habitat surveys using the classification system described by Bisson and others (2006), which is a modification of an earlier hierarchical subdivision of channel units by Hawkins and others (1993). Using this system, we classified habitat units into pools and non-pools. We conducted daily visual distance calibrations for personnel with a measuring tape. On the basis of these visual estimates, we recorded the length and width of each habitat unit. We also measured maximum and mean water depths, and visually estimated the percent total instream and overhead cover by cover type (for example, large and small wood, substrate, and undercut bank), and percent riparian shade provided by trees and shrubs. Global positioning system (GPS) location coordinates and altitudes were recorded at the beginning and end of the survey each day. Stream temperature data were collected with a handheld thermometer at all electrofishing sites — in the morning, at mid-day, and in the afternoon (appendix table A1) — to ensure that temperatures were appropriate for electrofishing or PIT tagging. Because of the high variability of water temperatures measured with handheld thermometers, owing to the time of year, time of day, weather, and proximity to springs, among other factors, this temperature information was not used in the analysis, but is provided in the appendix. Stream temperatures also were recorded by the BLM via a network of automated thermographs placed at various sites throughout the East and West Forks Jarbidge Rivers; this temperature information was used in the analysis.

Seven streamflow monitoring stations were established near the PIT tag interrogation system (PTIS) sites for the purposes of this study. Stream discharge measurements were made at each of these stations three times in August 2007 to assess tributary contributions to overall flow. Following the protocol of Bain and Stevenson (1999), we anchored a measuring tape perpendicular to streamflow and recorded the distance to the left and right wetted edge. We measured water depth and velocity with a Marsh-McBirney model 2000 flow meter at a minimum of 10 (although usually at about 20) intervals along the measuring tape. Because water depths were always less than 1 m, water velocities were measured at 60% of the depth at each interval.

PIT Tag Interrogation Systems

On September 15, 2006, we installed instream PTISs at three locations: at the mouth of Jack Creek; in West Fork Jarbidge River about 2.4 km downstream of Jack Creek; and in East Fork Jarbidge River near the town of Murphy Hot Springs, Idaho (fig. 1). At Jack Creek, one PIT tag transceiver (model FS2001F-ISO, Digital Angel, St. Paul, MN, USA) with a single custom antenna was installed. This site was powered by one 12-volt battery, which was trickle-charged by a solar panel. On the West Fork Jarbidge River, we installed two stream-width, pass-by antennas connected to a multiplexing transceiver (model FS1001M (MUX), Digital Angel, St. Paul, Minn., USA). The transceiver was powered by four 12-volt batteries, which were trickle-charged by two solar panels. The design of the PTIS in the East Fork Jarbidge River was similar to that in the West Fork Jarbidge River, but with two arrays of two pass-through antennas installed. The multiple-antenna design system, which was used and is described by Connolly and others (2005), was expected to provide high detection efficiencies; however, the systems installed for this project had two arrays instead of three, which would reduce the detection efficiencies as well as the ability to calculate them (Connolly and others, 2008). Data from the PTISs were downloaded and the batteries were changed once a week from September through December 2006, after which the equipment was removed for the winter.

In 2007, six PTISs were installed, three at the pre-established (in 2006) sites and three at new sites. On April 28, 2007, the three PTISs described above were reinstalled (fig. 1). In Dave Creek, on May 23, 2007, at about rkm 0.4, a single-antenna PTIS was installed similar to the one in Jack Creek. In the West Fork Jarbidge River, a MUX-style PTIS was installed on July 16, 2007, at the confluence of Pine Creek (rkm 26.2), with two stream-width antennas in Pine Creek and two in the West Fork Jarbidge River just downstream of the confluence. At the confluence of the East Fork and West Fork Jarbidge River ("the Forks"), another PTIS was installed on July 17, 2007. This system was comprised of two stream-width antennas in both the East Fork and West Fork Jarbidge River. To prevent damage to the PTIS equipment during winter, the units were removed from all sites on December 19, 2007. In general, the PTISs were strategically placed to investigate the potential linkage between local populations of fish throughout the watershed. In both years, the systems were tested with a test tag when battery exchanges or data downloading occurred.

Data Reconciliation and Analysis

Detections of PIT tagged fish were merged with tagging data. We used independent reconciliation of PIT tag records by two biologists to classify movements as upstream, downstream, or of unknown direction. The time and location of tagging and other interrogation events were used to determine the direction of fish movements. If multiple interrogation events of the same fish occurred within 2 days, they were considered to be one movement event. Directional fish movement events were accepted when there was consensus on the direction of movement by the two biologists. If discrepancies in assigning direction could not be reconciled, the movement was recorded as an unknown direction. The operational run times for the systems were determined using the buffer data (see below) and the field log notebooks of the PTIS units. The buffer data provided records of the dates and times that each interrogation system was running. Additional information was obtained by reviewing the field notes, which were recorded during downloading.

Recaptured bull trout were used to calculate information on movement and growth rates. Annual growth rates were calculated for all recaptured fish with more than 320 days between tagging and recapture. Because the number of days between tagging and recapture varied among individuals and between fish in different streams, the annual growth rate was standardized to a full year by dividing the change in length by the fraction of the year between capture and recapture. We conducted length frequency analysis to determine fish age at length for age-0 to age-2 bull trout. The length frequency histograms exhibit distinct modes of the first few age classes, which can provide insight into annual growth rates. The growth rate from length frequency analysis was validated with growth rates calculated via recaptured PIT tagged fish.

For our mark recapture study, we estimated the number of bull trout in two sections of Jack Creek as follows:

$$N = [(M + 1)*(C + 1)/ R + 1] - 1, \tag{1}$$

where M = number of fish marked on the first sample, C = number of fish captured in the second sample, and R = number of fish with a mark captured in the second sample. The confidence interval for each estimate was calculated using a binomial distribution when R/C was greater than 0.10 (Seber, 1982).

To estimate discharge at our streamflow monitoring stations, flow was computed by summing the flows of intervals, where the flow at each interval was calculated using the equation:

$$Q_n = d_n \times \left(\frac{b_{n+1} - b_{n-1}}{2} \right) \times v_n, \tag{2}$$

where Q_n = discharge at interval n, d_n = water depth at interval n, b_n = distance along the tape measure from the left wetted edge to point n, and v_n = mean velocity in interval n.

Results of Surveys

From July 19 to October 4, 2006, we sampled a total of 39.9 km of stream channel in reaches of East Fork and West Fork Jarbidge River, and in Fall, Slide, Dave, Jack, and Pine Creeks (figs. 2 and 3). A total of 349 bull trout were captured, of which 322 were PIT tagged and 237 were fin clipped for genetic analysis by the USFWS (table 1). The majority (84%) of fish were PIT tagged in Dave Creek, West Fork Jarbidge River, and Jack Creek. We collected only a few age-0 bull trout — three in upper Jack Creek, two in upper West Fork Jarbidge River, and one in Pine Creek. Sampling ended because of observed spawning activity by fish in Dave (August 6), Slide (August 22), and Jack (September 11) Creeks. We observed no direct bull trout mortalities during sampling in 2006.

From June 13 to September 14, 2007, we sampled 24.9 km of stream channel in the West Fork Jarbidge River and its tributaries, and 18 km of stream channel in the East Fork Jarbidge River and its tributaries (tables 2 and 3). The total lengths of stream sampled and latitude and longitude of the start and end points are shown in tables 4 and 5. In 2007, 1,353 bull trout were captured, of which 1,214 were PIT tagged, and 569 were fin clipped for genetic analysis (tables 2 and 3). The majority (88%) of bull trout were PIT tagged in upper East Fork Jarbidge River, upper West Fork Jarbidge River, and Dave, Pine, and Jack Creeks. We collected substantially more age-0 fish in 2007 than in 2006 — four fish in upper Dave Creek, 41 fish in Jack Creek,

36 fish in Pine Creek, and a single 28-mm bull trout collected on June 22, 2007, in the upper West Fork Jarbidge River. Three fish died as a consequence of electrofishing (direct mortality) in 2007, which was 0.2% of the total number of bull trout handled.

In addition to bull trout, redband trout, sculpin (*Cottus* spp.), and mountain whitefish (*Prosopium williamsoni*) were commonly encountered during sampling. In 2006, in the lower East Fork Jarbidge River just upstream of Murphy Hot Springs, we also encountered dace (*Rhinichthys* spp.), bridgelip sucker (*Catostomus columbianus*), and redside shiner (*Richardsonius balteatus*). We found no evidence of disease or introgression (vermiculation and pigment on the dorsal fin) with brook trout (*Salvelinus fontinalis*) in any of the bull trout we captured.

West Fork Jarbidge River watershed

West Fork Jarbidge River.—In 2006, one bull trout was captured near the West Fork Jarbidge River antenna site (rkm 14.5–15.5), and 96 fish were captured between rkm 22.0–30.0 (table 1). Sampling was stopped 1.3 km downstream of the end of fish distribution (as determined in 2007) due to time constraints. In 2007, sampling started at the first bridge upstream of the town of Jarbidge (rkm 21.7) and ended at rkm 32.2, 100 m upstream of a 1.3-m barrier falls, which was the uppermost point of fish distribution, as indicated by our sampling. We also sampled about a 100-m long reach of Sawmill Creek (which contributed 25% of the total West Fork Jarbidge River flow) and captured one redband trout and no bull trout. Several temporary, naturally formed low-flow fish barriers (substrate and wood) were present in West Fork Jarbidge River in 2007, with the most downstream barrier about 1.5 km upstream of the confluence with Pine Creek. In 2007, 272 bull trout were captured between rkm 21.7 and 32.2 (table 2, fig. 2). For both years, the minimum fork length was 23 mm, and the maximum was 330 mm (table 6). Most of the bull trout were age-1 and age-2, with relatively few fish longer than 200 mm (11% of our catch in 2006, 7% in 2007; table 6, fig. 4).

In 2007, we recaptured six bull trout that were originally PIT tagged in July and August 2006. The mean annual growth rate of these fish was 32 mm (range = 8-39 mm; SD = 4.8; fig. 4). The length of these fish at tagging ranged from 90 to 185 mm. Using length-frequency analysis, we estimated age-1 bull trout to be between 83 and 115 mm and age-2 fish to be longer than 120 mm in late July and early August 2006. In June 2007, age-1 bull trout were between 70 and 115 mm, and age-2 fish were from 120 to about 160 mm.

In both years, bull trout were found primarily at altitudes above 2,100 m and in greater abundance at increasingly greater altitudes (figs. 5 and 6). Redband trout were found throughout the area we sampled, but with reduced abundances as altitude increased. In 2006, bull trout longer than 200 mm were more common in the lower altitude reaches than in the higher reaches, but they were more evenly distributed in 2007. We sampled earlier in 2007 (June–July) than in 2006 (July–September), which could account for the differences in fish distribution. We sampled earlier in the year in 2007 because we encountered spawning activity during our sampling in 2006. A single age-0 bull trout was collected in the West Fork Jarbidge River in each year (figs. 4, 5, and 6). These fish were collected in the uppermost reaches, at altitudes greater than 2,100 m (figs. 5 and 6).

Of the 12,586 m of stream channel surveyed in 2006, 21% of the habitat units contained at least one bull trout. In 2006, 20% of the bull trout were found in pools and 16% of the habitat length we surveyed was pool habitat (table 7). In 2007, 50% of the habitat units surveyed contained at least one bull trout. Fifteen percent of these fish were found in pools and 12% of the habitat length we surveyed was pool habitat (table 7). In 2007, the upper end of our sampling was located higher in the basin (fig. 2), which may account for the greater number of habitat units containing bull trout.

Pine Creek.—Sampling in Pine Creek in both years began at the confluence of Pine Creek and West Fork Jarbidge River (fig. 2). In July 2006, about 5.5 km of stream habitat were sampled, with the exception of about 1.8 km of middle Pine Creek. In August 2007, sampling was continuous over 5.9 km of stream, but stopped about 200 m downstream of the end of fish distribution (as assessed by visual survey). In 2006, 27 bull trout were captured and 25 were PIT tagged (table 1). In 2007, 430 bull trout were captured, of which 380 were PIT tagged (table 2). Fish lengths ranged from 39 to 387 mm (table 6) and most were age-1, as determined from length frequencies (fig. 7). In both years, we captured only a few bull trout longer than 200 mm (table 6, fig. 7).

In 2007, we recaptured two bull trout that were originally PIT tagged in July 2006. The lengths of these fish at tagging were 108 and 162 mm and their annual growth rates were 57 and 35 mm (adjusted to 1 year), respectively, with 397 days between tagging and recapture (fig. 7). In 2006, one age-0 (39 mm) bull trout was captured and age-1 fish were between 100 and 130 mm, as determined from length frequency analysis (fig. 7). Age-0 bull trout captured in August 2007 ranged between 55 and 68 mm, and age-1 fish were from 99 to 155 mm in length (fig. 7).

In both years, bull trout were found mostly above 2,100 m altitude and in greater numbers and at higher abundances as altitude increased (figs. 8 and 9). Redband trout were found throughout the reaches sampled, but with reduced abundances in the highest altitudes. The middle reach of Pine Creek, which we did not sample in 2006, had the highest abundances of bull trout in 2007, with bull trout >200 mm long common. In 2006, only one age-0 bull trout was collected, whereas in 2007, several age-0 fish were captured in the reaches above 2,187 m altitude; figs. 7, 8, and 9). The highest altitude reaches had age-0 bull trout and redband trout present and relatively high abundances of bull trout overall.

Only 14% of the habitat units surveyed in 2006 contained bull trout, but 83% of habitat units contained at least one bull trout in 2007. This discrepancy probably was due to more extensive sampling in the middle and upper reaches of Pine Creek in 2007. In 2007, about 10% of the bull trout were found in pools, though only 9% of the stream length sampled was pool habitat (table 7).

Jack Creek.—In both years, sampling in Jack Creek began near the confluence with the West Fork Jarbidge River (fig. 2). In 2006, sampling began 20 m upstream of the PTIS (rkm 0.1) and continued to about rkm 4.3. We stopped sampling near this area because of fish spawning activity. On September 11, 2006, two pair of post-spawn bull trout were collected and several redds were observed. In 2007, our sampling began at the mouth of Jack Creek, continued to rkm 5.9, and included a mark-recapture population estimate presented below. This sampling extended about 100 m past the uppermost distribution of fish, which appears to end at a small waterfall with a 60 m bedrock slide downstream. On September 11, 2007, 0.8 km of stream was sampled above the presumed end of fish distribution, and no fish were observed. In early September 2006, 66 of the 70 bull trout captured were PIT tagged (table 1). In early August 2007, 101 of the 146 bull trout captured were PIT tagged (table 2, fig. 2). The minimum fork length was 61 mm in

2006 and 42 mm in 2007, and the maximum fork length was 310 and 283 mm (table 6), respectively. Most of the bull trout were age-1, with small percentages larger than 200 mm (11% in 2006, 10% in 2007; table 6, fig. 10).

We recaptured 10 bull trout in August 2007 that were originally PIT tagged in September 2006. The length of these fish at tagging ranged from 125 to 235 mm. The mean annual growth rate of these fish was 34 mm (range = 21–44 mm; SD = 4.8; fig. 10). Using length-frequency analysis, we determined that age-0 fish were less than 69 mm in early September 2006, age-1 bull trout were 115–142 mm, and age-2 bull trout were larger than 145 mm (fig. 10). In August 2007, age-0 bull trout were 42–62 mm, age-1 fish were 980–140 mm, and age-2 fish were 145–190 mm (fig. 10).

Consistent with findings in other streams in the upper Jarbidge River watershed, bull trout generally were found in greater numbers and at higher abundances at altitudes above 2,100 m and in greater numbers and at higher abundances as altitude increased (figs. 11 and 12). Redband trout were found in high abundances in lower Jack Creek below about 2,100 m altitude. Bull trout presence extended 500–600 m upstream of the last observed redband trout in both years in Jack Creek. In 2006, bull trout longer than 200 mm were found in the middle and upper portions of Jack Creek (fig. 11), but in 2007, fish of this size were found only in one area, at rkm 4.0 (fig. 12). In 2006, age-0 bull trout were found only at altitudes greater than 2,000 m. In 2007, however, age-0 bull trout were found about 0.5 km from the confluence, at about rkm 2.2, and also at rkm 4.2 near the high abundance of age-1 or older bull trout.

Of the 5.2 km of Jack Creek surveyed in 2006, 29% of the habitat units contained at least one bull trout. Although only 10% of the stream length surveyed was pool habitat (table 7), 44% of the bull trout captured were in pools. In 2007, we surveyed 5.4 km of stream and 45% of the habitat units contained at least one bull trout. We captured 39% of the bull trout in pools, while only 8% of the length of stream was pool habitat (table 7).

Deer Creek.—On September 10, 2007, we sampled Deer Creek from about rkm 6.9 to 9.4. Several small redband trout were observed, but not counted. No bull trout were observed. The riparian vegetation in the reach sampled was very sparse. The stream had a mean depth of 5 cm and very limited pool habitat.

Buck Creek.—We sampled two short reaches of Buck Creek (from about rkm 3.6–3.8 and rkm 12.7–13.1) on September 14, 2007. The habitat in Buck Creek was similar to that in Deer Creek. It was about 7 cm deep, lacked defined pools, and had sparse riparian vegetation. In general, the stream had very low velocity, heavy siltation, and high turbidity. Redband trout were abundant; however, no bull trout were observed.

East Fork Jarbidge River Watershed

East Fork Jarbidge River.—In 2006, we sampled near the East Fork Jarbidge River antenna site (rkm 4.1–4.9) on October 3 and in the wilderness area upstream of the East Fork Jarbidge River/Slide Creek confluence (rkm 15.6) from August 17–19 (fig. 3). No bull trout were captured near the antenna site, but 13 were captured between rkm 16.6 and 24.7 (table 1). Sampling stopped at rkm 24.7 due to time constraints. We sampled the East Fork Jarbidge River (rkm 32.5–35.0) from July 12–14, 2007, and captured 323 bull trout, of which 312 were PIT tagged (table 3, fig. 3). We also sampled 250 m of an unnamed tributary at about rkm 33.5. Redband trout were absent, but 13 bull trout, ranging from 130 to 238 mm, were captured in this tributary (table 3, fig. 16). We encountered a 2.5-m-high falls with no plunge pool 250 m upstream of the mouth of the unnamed tributary. We sampled an additional 50-m reach upstream of this barrier and found no fish. On the mainstem East Fork Jarbidge River below the confluence of Slide Creek, we recaptured one bull trout on July 17, 2007, that was originally tagged in Fall Creek in August 2006 (table 3, fig. 3). We stopped sampling in 2007 at approximately rkm 35.0 due to time constraints. Visual surveys indicated that fish were likely present for at least another 0.5 km upstream of our end point based on habitat conditions and water quantity. However, this survey was brief and no fish were directly observed.

The maximum size of fish tended to be larger in the upper East Fork Jarbidge River than anywhere else we sampled. In 2006, bull trout ranged in length from 135 to 260 mm (table 6) and in 2007 from 78 to 400 mm (table 6). Most of the fish we captured were age-3 or older, with a relatively high proportion of fish longer than 200 mm (38% in 2006; 19% in 2007) (table 6, fig. 13). From length-frequency analysis, we determined that age-1 bull trout were between 78 to 100 mm, age-2 bull trout were between 107 and 143 mm, and age-3 bull trout were 143 mm and longer in mid-July 2007 (fig. 13). The sample size was too small in 2006 to determine age classes. No age-0 bull trout were observed in the East Fork Jarbidge River during 2006 or 2007.

In 2006, bull trout were uncommon but increased in abundance at altitudes above 2,100 m near the upstream end of our survey (fig. 14). Redband trout were abundant throughout the area sampled in 2006. In 2007, bull trout were present at the downstream end of our sampling (fig. 15), were numerically dominant at about 2,290 m altitude, and were the only salmonid present above 2,320 m altitude. Bull trout abundance decreased upstream of the East Fork Jarbidge River confluence with an unnamed tributary and spring at rkm 33.5. In this area, stream depths were very shallow and the stream contained no surface flow for about 100 m. Surface flow and high numbers of bull trout were present upstream of the no-flow section and the channel substrate primarily was bedrock. On July 14, 2007, the last day of sampling the upper East Fork Jarbidge River, bull trout were the only salmonid present and were relatively abundant. We speculate that high abundance of bull trout continued at least another 0.5 km upstream as no barriers were present.

In 2007, we recaptured a large bull trout (400 mm) at our lowermost sampling site in the East Fork Jarbidge River (fig. 3). This same fish was originally tagged in Fall Creek (see appendix, fig. A49) and had grown 40 mm and nearly doubled its weight in 331 days (440.6 to 767.2 g, table 6). We recaptured no other PIT tagged fish in 2006 from the East Fork Jarbidge River.

We surveyed 8 km of the East Fork Jarbidge River in 2006 and only 5% of the habitat units contained bull trout. We found 25% of the bull trout in pools, while 19% of the length sampled was pool habitat (table 7). In 2007, the survey in the East Fork Jarbidge River covered a higher altitude reach except for a short 0.4-km reach at the East Fork Jarbidge River/ Slide Creek confluence (fig. 3) and 52% of the habitat units sampled had bull trout (table 7). Nineteen percent of the bull trout we captured were in pools, while 13% of the stream length sampled was pool habitat.

Cougar Creek.—We sampled Cougar Creek on July 11–12, 2007, starting at the confluence with the East Fork Jarbidge River and continuing upstream 0.7 km; no bull trout were observed in this reach (table 3 and fig. 3). Several temporary, low-flow fish barriers (mostly substrate and wood) were present. From about rkm 1.2–1.5, we captured one bull trout that was 138 mm long. From rkm 1.8 to the limit of fish presence at rkm 3.1, we caught six bull trout, ranging in length from 180 to 340 mm (table 6, figs. 16 and 17). Here, the substrate was bedrock and the stream had a steep gradient above 2,100 m altitude. Although there were several cascading waterfalls and slides in this section, redband trout were relatively abundant. The end of fish distribution was a 2.5-m-high falls; we electrofished upstream of these falls an additional 100 m, but no fish were observed. Cougar Creek was not sampled in 2006. Only 4% of the habitat units contained bull trout in Cougar Creek, and five of the seven bull trout we caught were in pools (table 7).

Fall Creek.—We sampled Fall Creek on August 20, 2006, starting at the confluence with the East Fork Jarbidge River and continuing upstream for about 2.0 km (fig. 3). On July 15, 2007, we sampled from rkm 1.4 to rkm 3.4, but did not find any fish upstream of rkm 3.2 (fig. 3). In 2006, we captured and PIT tagged nine bull trout (table 1). In 2007, 30 bull trout were captured and PIT tagged (table 3). The combined range of lengths of fish from both years was 79–360 mm (table 6). Most of the bull trout in 2007 were age-1, with only a few age-2 fish present (fig. 18). The sample size of fish in 2006 was too small for age determinations. One bull trout longer than 200 mm that was PIT tagged in 2006 was subsequently recaptured in 2007 in the mainstem East Fork Jarbidge River (rkm 23.5) near the confluence with Slide Creek, about 2.5 km from the tagging site.

In 2006, bull trout were uncommon from the confluence with the East Fork Jarbidge River to about 1.0 km upstream (fig. 19). In 2007, bull trout were found with increasing frequency and abundance in the higher altitudes sampled (fig. 20). Four bull trout longer than 200 mm were caught near the end of fish distribution (fig. 20). All size classes of redband trout were found throughout the length of stream sampled in 2006. In 2007, redband trout abundance decreased in the upper reaches of Fall Creek, and bull trout were the only salmonid present in the final 130 m of stream below a barrier waterfall.

Of the 2.0 km of Fall Creek surveyed in 2006, only 8% of the habitat units contained bull trout. Twenty-two percent of the catch was from pools, and 14% of the stream length was pool habitat. Of the 1.8 km of stream sampled in 2007, 28% of the habitat units contained at least one bull trout, with 20% of the fish found in pools. Only 9% of the stream length sampled was pool habitat (table 7).

Slide Creek.—On August 21, 2006, we sampled Slide Creek from its confluence with the East Fork Jarbidge River upstream to rkm 5.5, where we observed spawning bull trout. We did not sample two small sections in 2006, one from rkm 2.9 to rkm 3.2 and another from rkm 4.6 to rkm 5.4 (table 1, fig. 3). On July 16, 2007, we sampled the creek from rkm 4.6 to rkm 7.7 (table 3 and fig. 3). In 2006, four bull trout were captured and PIT tagged (table 1) and in 2007, only three fish were captured and PIT tagged (table 3). The length of bull trout ranged from 189 to 300 mm in 2006 and from 95 to 220 mm in 2007 (table 6 and fig. 21). On August 22, 2006, we observed two gravid bull trout (300 and 190 mm) and another spawning pair and therefore stopped sampling. In 2006, all four of the bull trout were captured at an altitude above 2,100 m (fig. 22). In 2007, two of the bull trout we caught were likely age-1 fish, on the basis of estimates of size at age from other fish in the East Fork Jarbidge River (fig. 21). The lengths of the few bull trout caught in 2007 varied widely, and the largest fish (220 mm) was caught very high in the watershed (fig. 23). No bull trout were caught in pools in either year (table 7, figs. 22 and 23). All size classes of redband trout were found throughout Slide Creek in 2006 and 2007. Sampling efficiency generally was less in Slide Creek relative to that in other streams due to narrow stream width and thick riparian vegetation.

Dave Creek.—In August 2006, we collected samples between rkm 6.8 and rkm 11.7 on Dave Creek and PIT tagged 111 of the 129 bull trout collected (table 1, fig. 3). We stopped sampling on August 6 because we encountered one sexually mature male bull trout and two bull trout paired together over spawning gravel. From June 28 through July 2, 2007, sampling started

11

at rkm 6.8 and ended 80 m upstream of the last fish observed (at about rkm 14.0). We also repeated sampling from rkm 10.5 to 13.9 on September 11, 2007, to recapture PIT tagged fish for estimating summer growth rates. From June 28 through July 2, 2007, 105 bull trout were captured and 100 of these were PIT tagged (table 3, fig. 3). In September, a total of 23 bull trout were captured and 11 were newly PIT tagged. Seven recaptured bull trout were originally PIT tagged during our June 2007 sampling and three bull trout were recaptures from 2006. During this time, we captured three sexually mature, male bull trout, ranging in length from 153 to 200 mm.

The lengths of bull trout captured from Dave Creek in 2006 ranged from 97 to 229 mm (table 6). Most of the fish were age-1, with a few being longer than 200 mm (12% of the total catch; table 6, fig. 24). In 2007, the lengths ranged from 59 to 232 mm, and only 5% of the fish were longer than 200 mm (table 6).

We recaptured three bull trout in Dave Creek during 2007 that were originally PIT tagged in 2006. These fish ranged from 108 to 114 mm at tagging and their mean annual growth rate was 37 mm (range = 35–39 mm; SD = 2.2; fig. 24). Using length frequency analysis, we determined age-1 bull trout fork lengths to range from 97 to 134 mm and age-2 fish ranged from 140 to 180 mm in early August 2006 (fig. 18). We also recaptured seven bull trout in September 2007 that were tagged in June 2007. The mean growth of these fish over 68 days was 11 mm (range: 1–22 mm). In late June 2007, the fork length of age-1 bull trout ranged from 83 to 127 mm and age-2 fish were estimated to be between 140 and 175 mm (fig. 24). In September 2007, we did not collect enough fish to make a length frequency analysis; however, we collected four bull trout fry that ranged in length from 59 to 66 mm.

In both years, bull trout were found in greater numbers and in higher abundances as altitude increased (figs. 25 and 26). Redband trout were present throughout Dave Creek, but abundance decreased at higher altitudes. In 2006, bull trout larger than 200 mm commonly were mixed with smaller fish (fig. 25). In 2007, however, bull trout larger than 200 mm primarily were found at high altitudes (fig. 26).

We surveyed 4.9 km of Dave Creek in 2006 and 46% of the habitat units contained bull trout. About 15% of the bull trout were found in pools and 7% of the length of stream sampled was pool habitat (table 7). In 2007, 62% of the habitat units had bull trout, 10% of the bull trout were found in pools, and only 2% of the survey length was pool habitat.

Overall Distribution and Abundance of Bull Trout in Jack Creek

In 2007, we estimated the population for age-1 or older bull trout in the fish-bearing portion (lower 5.3 km) of Jack Creek. Because of the low number of bull trout captured in the lower section of Jack Creek (downstream of Jenny Creek, n=6, with 2 recaptured bull trout), we did not calculate a population estimate in that section. In the 3.6 km upstream of Jenny Creek, we captured and marked 66 bull trout during our first effort, and during our second effort, 23 of the 52 fish collected had marks from the initial sampling. This yielded a population estimate of 153 bull trout (SD = 17.5; CV = 11.9; 95% CI = 114–220). During our recapture efforts in upper Jack Creek, we collected 35% of the fish tagged the day before. In our recapture efforts in lower Jack Creek, we collected 33% of the fish tagged the day before. This indicates that our one-pass electrofishing effort had a catchability of 35% over the 5.3 km of stream.

For the streams in which bull trout were present, regression analysis indicated a significant correlation ($P < 0.001$, $R^2 = 0.06$) between bull trout abundance and altitude. We also found a highly significant correlation ($P < 0.001$, $R^2 = 0.01$) between the number of bull trout (per m) and pool depth. The low R^2 values indicate that although altitude and pool depth have a significant relationship to bull trout abundance, they explain only a small amount of the variation. We should make clear that bull trout abundance was relative because we conducted only a single upstream sampling pass with no block nets, and capture efficiency was variable due to several factors (temperature, light, crew experience, substrate, for example). No other relations were evident between the relative abundance of bull trout and other habitat features that were quantified, such as pool cover (large and small wood, substrate, and undercut bank), riparian shade, and wetted width.

Movements of Bull Trout

In 2006, the PTISs at West Fork Jarbidge River (rkm 15.0), East Fork Jarbidge River (rkm 4.1), and Jack Creek (rkm 0.1) were operated from September 15 to December 18, 2006, when they were removed for the winter. During that time, five bull trout were detected moving downstream at the West Fork Jarbidge River site, with one of these fish first detected by the PTIS in Jack Creek (table 8; figs. A3, A14, A26, and A28). Three of the five fish were tagged in the West Fork Jarbidge River, one was tagged in Pine Creek, and one in Jack Creek. All fish were detected moving downstream after October 7, 2006 (figs. A3, A14, A26, A28, and A30). We detected no fish on the PTIS at the East Fork Jarbidge River site.

In 2007, we re-installed and operated the PTISs in the West Fork Jarbidge River, East Fork Jarbidge River, and Jack Creek and also installed a system in Dave Creek, at the confluences of the West Fork Jarbidge River and Pine Creek and the East Fork Jarbidge River and West Fork Jarbidge River at the Forks (table 8). All systems were operated from April to mid-December. Although the single antenna systems in Jack and Dave Creeks were intermittently affected by antenna noise that may have reduced their detection efficiency (fig. 27), test tags passed weekly through these systems indicated no such loss in efficiency. The larger MUX systems were, in general, fully operational (fig. 27), but some conditions, such as low battery power, electronics malfunctions, and extreme temperatures may have reduced their detection efficiency. Maintaining an adequate battery voltage, by charging with solar power or replacing batteries, was difficult as winter approached because of the remote location combined with decreased sunlight and temperatures.

Three upstream and four downstream directional movements of bull trout were detected at the PTIS on the East Fork Jarbidge River at Murphy Hot Springs or the East Fork and West Fork PTIS antennas at the Forks (fig. 28). In both years, the majority (83%) of fish interrogated at the three PTISs in the West Fork Jarbidge River were moving downstream (fig. 29). However, two fish moved upstream in Jack Creek and one fish moved upstream at the mainstem West Fork Jarbidge River PTIS at rkm 15. The upstream movements of fish in Jack Creek occurred in late spring as the main West Fork Jarbidge River approached base flows and water temperatures increased.

Appendix figures A1 through A50 show all data for fish interrogated in 2006 and 2007, and fish that showed evidence of movement by recapture. There were 44 new interrogations of PIT tagged bull trout in 2007 (table 8), and one fish from Jack Creek that was interrogated in both 2006 and 2007 (fig. A3). Most fish that were detected were tagged in the West Fork Jarbidge River or its tributaries, but two fish were tagged in Dave Creek. In Dave Creek, one fish

(195 mm) was tagged in August 2006 and detected on April 29, 2007, at the PTIS in the East Fork Jarbidge River at Murphy Hot Springs. The other bull trout (164 mm) was tagged in Dave Creek on June 28, 2007, and detected at both the East Fork and West Fork PTIS antennas at the Forks on July 28, 2007, but this fish was not detected at the PTIS on Dave Creek (installed on May 23, 2007) or the PTIS on the East Fork Jarbidge River at Murphy Hot Springs (figs. A1 and A2). Both of these fish were tagged in a similar location.

Bull trout in Jack Creek showed several movement patterns, with fish tagged at relatively high altitudes in the drainage basin leaving the creek and inhabiting the West Fork Jarbidge River, the East Fork Jarbidge River, and presumably the mainstem below the Forks. In 2007, only two bull trout were detected by the PTIS in the West Fork Jarbidge River (rkm 15), and they were tagged in Jack Creek (table 8). Fish tagged in the upper reaches of Jack Creek tended to emigrate in mid-July (figs. A4 through A8 and A10). For example, one bull trout (175 mm) tagged near the upper end of fish distribution in 2006 was detected moving out of Jack Creek on July 13, 2007. This fish was detected moving past the PTIS at the Forks on November 20, 2007 (fig. A6). Another bull trout (138 mm) tagged in the upper reaches was detected on the Jack Creek PTIS on July 21, 2007. This fish was then detected 2 days later moving downstream through the PTIS at the Forks (fig. A7). Two fish (138 and 171 mm), tagged in the lower sections of Jack Creek in early August 2007, were detected emigrating from the creek in November 2007 (figs. A11 and A12). Finally, one bull trout tagged in the upper reaches of Jack Creek in September 2006 was detected on the PTIS at the East Fork Jarbidge River at Murphy Hot Springs moving downstream on August 26, 2007, and was detected later on October 19, 2008, in the West Fork Jarbidge River at the Forks moving upstream (fig. A9)

The PTIS at the confluence of the West Fork Jarbidge River and Pine Creek had many more fish detections than any of the other PTIS locations (table 8). Fish tagged in the upper West Fork Jarbidge River had the highest number of interrogations, with 20 fish detected at the West Fork Jarbidge River/Pine Creek site (table 8). Ninety percent of these fish were moving down the West Fork Jarbidge River from September through November (fig. 29). Ten of the fish tagged in the West Fork Jarbidge River were detected or recaptured in Pine Creek, indicating a relatively high degree of connectivity between these watersheds (figs. A21, A22, A24, A25, A27, A35, A39, A42, A44, and A48). We detected eight fish at the West Fork Jarbidge River/Pine Creek site that were tagged in Pine Creek, seven of which were emigrating downstream between October 7 and November 4, 2007. The eighth fish was detected moving downstream at the same time of year on November 3, 2006, at the PTIS on the West Fork Jarbidge River (rkm 15), however, the PTIS at West Fork Jarbidge River/Pine Creek (rkm 26.2) was not established until 2007 (fig. A14). Bull trout were detected at the West Fork Jarbidge River/Pine Creek site continuously during the summer and detections decreased as winter approached (fig. 29). Bull trout were detected at the interrogation systems nearly all hours of the day, but with a higher frequency during the night (fig. 30).

Distribution, Growth, and Movement of Bull Trout

Findings from the 2006 and 2007 electrofishing surveys suggest that bull trout populations with recruitment to age-1 fish occurred in Pine, Jack, Dave, and Fall Creeks as well as the West Fork and East Fork of the Jarbidge River at altitudes above 2,100 m. Few bull trout were observed in Cougar and Slide Creeks, indicating that stable reproductive populations were not present in those creeks at the time of the survey. The results of the genetic analysis reporting on the relatedness between sub-populations of bull trout from the streams described above were highly supportive of our distribution and movement findings and can be found in DeHaan and others (2007). No bull trout were found in Deer and Buck Creeks, however, migratory bull trout may inhabit those streams intermittently.

General Catch Information and Population Characteristics

During 2 years of sampling in the upper Jarbidge River watershed, we captured 1,702 bull trout (80% of which were captured in 2007) and counted more than 4,000 redband trout in pools only. Bull trout were found primarily at altitudes above 2,100 m (87% of all those encountered), which was consistent with the findings in other studies that the distribution of juvenile bull trout within streams was strongly associated with altitude (Dunham and Rieman, 1999; Paul and Post, 2001; Dunham and others, 2003a; Ripley and others, 2005).

Redband trout were found in all areas where bull trout were sampled, except in the upper reaches of fish distribution in East Fork Jarbidge River and Jack Creek, where bull trout were the only salmonid present. In streams with notable bull trout populations (such as the headwaters of the East Fork and West Fork Jarbidge River, and Dave, Fall, Pine, and Jack Creeks), the relative abundance of redband trout decreased as the upper limit of fish distribution was approached. The relative abundance of bull trout tended to increase and that of redband trout decreased with increasing altitude. One explanation for the change in numerical dominance of bull trout over redband trout with altitude is that altitude can serve as a surrogate for stream temperature (Dunham and others, 2003b; Rieman and others, 2007). In upper reaches of those studies, most streams had an abundance of cobble and boulder substrates with interstitial spaces for cover, and relatively cool temperatures, conditions typical of good bull trout habitat in other streams (Fraley and Shepard 1989; Rieman and others, 2007). The ability of bull trout to dominate the upper, higher altitude reaches of streams could be due to their superiority in interspecific interactions, and may be an example of biotic resistance exerted by bull trout (Elton, 1958). Biotic resistance through predation, which can contribute to invasion or colonization resistance (Harvey and others, 2004; Ward and others 2008), seems probable given the highly piscivorous nature of bull trout (Fraley and Shepard, 1989; Donald and Alger, 1993).

The distribution of bull trout and redband trout in streams of the Jarbidge River basin could change if temperatures increase due to climate change or other factors. For example, increasing stream temperatures could favor redband trout, leading to an expansion of their distribution, restricted distributions of bull trout, and a decrease in the competitive ability of bull trout (Rieman and others, 2007). When bull trout distributions become restricted, they may be unable to reclaim dominance to their full historical range because of biotic resistance from redband trout occupying those reaches. In short, on the basis of potentially higher stream temperatures alone, more habitat would be suitable for redband trout and less for bull trout. The area of transition in dominance of bull trout over redband trout, however, may be an important aspect to monitor relative to the sustainability of bull trout in the Jarbidge River watershed.

Using a mark-recapture procedure, we estimated that there were about 153 bull trout in Jack Creek upstream of Jenny Creek (95% CI = 114 – 220). Our estimate was similar to that of a single pass survey by NDOW, which reported about 102 bull trout for the entire Jack Creek in 2002 (Johnson, 2002). From the mark-recapture data, our one-pass capture efficiency was estimated to be 35%, and methods similar to ours could be used to evaluate changes in bull trout abundance over time in Jack Creek. In fact, estimating the abundance of bull trout in Jack Creek could become a routine method for status and trends monitoring in the Jarbidge River basin. We do not, however, recommend extrapolating our sampling efficiency estimate from Jack Creek to other streams to estimate fish abundance by simply dividing the number of fish captured in a stream by 0.35 to obtain an estimate of abundance. Electrofishing sampling efficiency can vary widely depending upon many factors, including crew experience, equipment type, fish size, fish abundance, stream width, stream flow, temperature, water clarity, cloud cover, and sun position (Zalewski and Cowx, 1990). It seems prudent to keep Jack Creek as a status and trends monitoring site for future bull trout population abundance estimates and perhaps to establish reference sites in other streams to monitor relative abundance.

Length-frequency distributions of bull trout in streams of the upper Jarbidge River watershed were generally similar and were dominated by age-1 and age-2 fish. This is indicative of good reproduction success and suggests that older bull trout might show a fluvial life history and therefore be absent from our sample. An exception to this conclusion was found in the upper East Fork Jarbidge River (sampled in 2007), which was dominated by age-3 or older fish, although it should be noted that the uppermost fish distribution was not reached and there may have been younger fish in this area. The dominance of older fish suggests that the numbers of age-1 and age-2 fish were suppressed by predation (cannibalism) or that younger fish emigrate to rear in the lower mainstem East Fork Jarbidge River or tributaries. Beauchamp and Van Tassell (2001) found that bull trout of all sizes were capable of eating fusiform prey fishes of up to 50% of their own total length. They also used model simulations and field data to show that cannibalism by bull trout could remove substantial proportions of age-0 and age-1 fish, but not age-2 or older fish in Lake Billy Chinook, Oregon. Diet analysis of piscivorous-sized bull trout would be required to confirm this notion in the upper East Fork Jarbidge River.

The length of age-1 bull trout varied temporally, ranging from 68 mm in the West Fork Jarbidge River on June 21, 2006, to 145 mm in Pine Creek on August 22, 2007, similar to fish in other basins, such as the Flathead River, Montana (Fraley and Shepard, 1989), Metolius River, Oregon (Ratliff, 1992), Kananaskis Lake in Alberta, Canada (Stelfox, 1997), and the Cedar River, Washington (M. Mesa, U.S. Geological Survey, unpub. data, 2008).

Age-0 bull trout probably did not begin to emerge until late June or later in most tributaries of the upper Jarbidge River watershed. We collected 5 age-0 bull trout in 2006 and 83 in 2007. Our sampling did not target age-0 fish; however, the lack of very small (< 30 mm) fish in our catches probably reflects the timing of our sampling and the low susceptibility of this portion of the age group to our sampling gear. Small fish are less vulnerable to capture by electrofishing than are larger fish, they are less visible to netters, and their body size facilitates hiding in interstitial spaces of the streambed material (Reynolds, 1983). Low numbers of age-0 bull trout observed in most streams was probably not a result of poor hatching success or low survival. However, given the high numbers of bull trout collected in the upper East Fork Jarbidge River and Fall Creek, we speculate that if age-0 fish were present at that time of year, we would have at least observed some of them.

By examining length-frequency distributions and assigning ages to the distinct modes, we estimated the age and growth rates for younger bull trout. This technique worked well for age-0 and age-1 fish, but not for older fish. The largest age-0 fish we collected was 69 mm and most age-1 fish were larger (range: 78–145 mm). It was more difficult to estimate the size ranges of age-2 or older bull trout because individual growth rates were highly variable and the age breaks between age-2 and age-3 fish were unclear. Recapturing PIT tagged bull trout allowed us to validate the age assignments of the length frequency histograms and to estimate the growth rates of older age classes.

Although the sample sizes of recaptured PIT tagged fish in any stream during our study were small, they were sufficient to provide some insight into annual growth rates. Of the 25 fish tagged in 2006 that were recaptured in 2007, 3 were from Dave Creek, 1 from East Fork Jarbidge River, 5 from Pine Creek, 6 from West Fork Jarbidge River, and 10 from Jack Creek. The mean annual growth rate was 36 mm for all recaptured bull trout (n = 23) and ranged from 32 mm in the West Fork Jarbidge River to 38 mm in Pine Creek. These mean annual growth rates compare favorably with those of bull trout in other areas, such as 28 mm in Trestle Creek, Idaho (Downs and others, 2006). There are several possible reasons for the low number of fish tagged in 2006 being recaptured later. First, because the number of tags deployed in 2006 was much fewer than in 2007, there were simply fewer tagged fish available in 2007 that were tagged in 2006. Second, our sampling in 2006 generally took place lower in the watersheds compared to our work in 2007, when we focused activity towards the upper end of fish distribution. Third, the probability of over-winter mortality of fish in the basin seems high (because of low winter flow, anchor ice formation, and relatively sparse abundance of deep pools in areas where bull trout were more common), which would reduce the recapture potential. It is possible that some shedding of PIT tags occurred. Although we tagged all bull trout greater than 120-mm fork length in the dorsal sinus to minimize tag loss, we do not know the rate of tag loss for bull trout tagged in this area. Dieterman and Hoxmeier (2009) found that brook trout and brown trout (*Salmo trutta*) tagged in the dorsal musculature had high tag retention rates—100% and 95%, respectively, over 2 months in small streams. Finally, there also is a possibility that tagged fish emigrated out of the area sampled in 2007. If this movement occurred when the PTISs were not operating, we would not be aware of it. All these factors could contribute to low recapture rates of PIT tagged bull trout on an annual basis.

There was no clear longitudinal gradient in fish size or propensity to emigrate as we progressed from downstream to upstream areas in the Jarbidge River watershed. Some studies have shown that fish become smaller with progression upstream, because fish size was related to stream depth observed at the habitat unit scale (see, for example, Patrick. 1975; Schlosser, 1982; Anderson, 1985). Hughes (1998) suggested, however, that this relationship does not always apply to drift-feeding stream salmonids. The lack of a longitudinal gradient in bull trout size in our streams was probably due to the relatively small size of our streams and that bull trout can show considerable intra-stream movements (see discussion below), which would help distribute fish of different sizes throughout the stream.

Movement of Bull Trout

In general, the PTISs were effective at detecting upstream and downstream movements of bull trout and documenting connectivity between headwater and mainstem areas. Bull trout were detected moving from upper ends of fish distribution in the West Fork Jarbidge River (n=13), Pine Creek (n=5), and Jack Creek (n=7) to the lower West Fork Jarbidge River below the confluence with Jack Creek. Fish from Jack (n=4) and Dave (n=1) Creeks were detected at the confluence of the East Fork and West Fork Jarbidge River. When the data on fish movements detected by the PTISs through December 2007 are combined, they indicate some degree of connectivity between headwater populations and the mainstem East Fork Jarbidge River and West Fork Jarbidge River.

There was a pulse of downstream movement of fish in October and November 2007 from Pine Creek, West Fork Jarbidge River (rkm 26), and Jack Creek, most likely associated with declining temperatures and a slight increase in flow. While downstream movements of fish at the

West Fork Jarbidge River and Pine Creek confluence PTIS (at rkm 26) peaked in October, downstream movement was detected at that site in all months that the PTIS was operating. Downstream movement by bull trout in the fall has been documented in other systems, including the Flathead River system in Montana (Muhlfeld and Marotz, 2005), the Boise River in Idaho (Monnot and others, 2008), Trestle Creek in Idaho (Downs and others, 2006), Grand Ronde River system in Oregon (Bellerud and others, 1997), and the Arrow Lakes region in British Columbia (McPhail and Murray, 1979). Bull trout in the Grand Ronde system were fluvial fish and those in the Flathead River, Boise River, Trestle Creek, and the Arrow Lakes region had adfluvial life histories. All these studies suggest that the autumn emigration of juvenile bull trout correlates with decreasing water temperatures. There also were some downstream movements of fish out of Jack Creek in mid-July with some of these fish detected moving down the West Fork Jarbidge River past the Forks within a few days, and some even entering the East Fork Jarbidge River. It appears that some bull trout, particularly from Jack Creek, migrate downstream of the Forks and inhabit the mainstem Jarbidge River, but the extent or duration of mainstem habitat use is unclear. In the Flathead River system, juvenile bull trout emigrated primarily from June through August (Fraley and Shepard, 1989).

Detections of upstream movement of bull trout were relatively rare (17% of all movement detected from PTISs) compared with detections of downstream movement. However, most of the fish we tagged were juvenile fish that may not become migratory for several years. Most of the upstream movements (62%) were detected at the Pine Creek and West Fork Jarbidge River confluence (rkm 26). These fish appeared to be moving back and forth, potentially rearing in the vicinity of the PTIS. Other upstream movements of fish were detected at PTISs at West Fork Jarbidge River (at rkm 15) and Jack Creek. These upstream movements occurred in June 2007 as the West Fork Jarbidge River flows were decreasing and water temperatures were increasing. Other investigators have found that peak upstream movements of fluvial bull trout in Montana's Blackfoot River occurred during the spring as water temperatures were increasing (Swanberg, 1997; Homel and Budy, 2008). These fish may have been on spawning migrations. As evidence of this, the largest bull trout tagged in Jack Creek (310 mm) out-migrated in October 2006 and returned the following June to Jack Creek (fig. A3). Seasonal movement of juvenile bull trout (upstream migrations in the spring and downstream in the fall) have been reported by others in Trestle Creek, Idaho (Downs and others, 2006) and South Fork Walla Walla River, Oregon (Homel and Budy, 2008). Continued operation of the PTISs in the Jarbidge River basin would allow for additional detections to confirm these life history trends for migrating fish.

Seasonal fish barriers, primarily downed wood and substrate, were present during low flows in the West Fork Jarbidge River upstream of Pine Creek and in lower Cougar Creek. Similar temporary barriers may form in any of the streams we sampled, may not be present every year, and likely form during low-flow conditions. Such conditions may prevent bull trout from reaching areas used for spawning or rearing, thus isolating some fish in tributaries intermittently. Because bull trout may access their spawning areas during low-flow conditions in the fall, these temporary barriers may decrease inter-annual distribution, but increase straying and gene flow among certain populations. This may be true of the bull trout in the upper West Fork Jarbidge River and Pine Creek populations as well as the Cougar Creek and East Fork Jarbidge River populations, although there was little evidence of juvenile recruitment in Cougar Creek during our survey.

Results from this and other studies (Fraley and Shepard, 1989; Rieman and MacIntyre 1993; Bellerud and others, 1997; Haas and McPhail, 2001) show substantial variation in migration behavior of bull trout, which is associated with many factors, including water temperatures, stream discharge, fish size, food availability, and spawning. Bull trout also can be highly migratory during non-spawning periods (Muhlfeld and others, 2003; Downs and others, 2006; Brenkman and others, 2007). The movements of bull trout in the Jarbidge River system indicate a high degree of connectivity between fish in different streams. Maintenance and potential enhancement of this connectivity will likely promote expression of important life history diversity (Muhlfeld and Marotz, 2005), which would contribute to the persistence of the population under varying habitat and climate conditions (Dunham and others, 2003a; Rieman and others, 2007).

Most of the bull trout (89%) emigrating downstream in the Jarbidge River basin were age-2 or older, with a few age-1 fish migrating from the West Fork Jarbidge River, Pine Creek, and Jack Creek. The fish detected at the PTISs tended to be the larger individuals within their age class. Although we cannot know the actual length of a tagged fish at the time of detection, we assumed that the size of fish at tagging was representative of its size relative to its cohort when detected. Our results were consistent with others describing an emigration of smaller bull trout (for example, Fraley and Shepard, 1989; Bellerud and others, 1997; Downs and others, 2006). Fraley and Shepard (1989) reported that 81% of the emigrating juvenile bull trout from the Flathead River system were ages 2 and 3. Mogen and Kaeding (2005) also observed that juvenile bull trout commenced migrations at age 2 or 3. Because larger fish may have a greater burst swim speed ability (Mesa and others, 2004), and would be less vulnerable to predation due to their larger size, migrating at a larger size could increase survival probability. A similar situation could exist in the Jarbidge River where emigrating at a relatively large size might have survival advantages and play a role in the persistence of a fluvial life history.

We were unable to estimate the efficiency and precision of the PTISs in the Jarbidge River basin because of their configuration or an insufficient number of detections. Too few detections were available to estimate detection efficiencies for the systems with multiple antenna arrays. Estimating antenna efficiencies in Dave or Jack Creeks was not possible because there was only one antenna at each site. However, the efficiency of any PTIS would vary over time and is influenced by stream discharge, the direction of fish movements, intermittency in PTIS operation due to low battery power, and malfunctioning electronics.

We maintained a reasonably good record of operation at the sites and continued to improve antenna anchoring and electronic system stability. Because our systems were based on the designs used by Connolly and others (2008) and the sizes of our streams were similar to those in their study, we surmise that detection efficiencies of our systems were good when the complete detection systems were intact. Their work showed that detection efficiencies of multiple antennas arranged in a series of arrays exceeded 96% under a variety of dynamic stream conditions. The systems tested by Connolly and others (2008) had three arrays, so that if any one array failed, two other arrays would still be able to determine the direction of fish movement and allow an estimate of detection efficiency. The systems in the Jarbidge River consisted of one or two arrays, and therefore had less redundancy, a reduced ability to determine the direction of movement or calculate detection efficiencies, and likely lower detection efficiencies than the systems described in Connolly and others (2008).

Conclusions, Summary, and Recommendations

Prior to the study described here, little was known about the bull trout population in the upper Jarbidge River basin, and biologists estimated that fewer than 500 bull trout were present within the core area defined by the U.S. Fish and Wildlife Service (2004). Our results indicate that almost four times that many bull trout inhabit the core area and that these fish show substantial movements between tributaries, increased abundance with increasing altitude, and growth rates indicative of a high-quality habitat. Our estimate of population size of bull trout in Jack Creek should provide a baseline that will allow managers to monitor changes in abundance over time. Further, our work included some information on the abundance of redband trout that provides an understanding of the distribution of these fish relative to that of bull trout. Collectively, our results provide new insight into the ecology and biology of bull trout in the upper Jarbidge River watershed that should prove useful for developing recovery actions and managing these fish.

Our research was successful in documenting some important population and movement characteristics of bull trout in the Jarbidge River basin. We documented the relative abundance of bull trout throughout the watershed, their annual and seasonal growth rates, the timing and magnitude of downstream migrations, and the timing of the onset of spawning. Bull trout were found primarily in the upper parts of tributaries at altitudes greater than 2,100 m and numerically dominated redband trout in the upper East Fork Jarbidge River and Jack Creek. Redband trout, however, were more numerous throughout the rest of the watershed. Bull trout from the upper East Fork Jarbidge River, upper West Fork Jarbidge River, and Dave, Jack, and Pine Creeks had length-frequency distributions indicative of healthy populations with good potential for growth in body size and number. The annual growth rates of individual bull trout in the basin ranged from 21 to 61 mm and were indicative of good habitat conditions and within the range reported for bull trout elsewhere. Although bull trout showed some downstream movement during the spring and summer, most of their emigration occurred in autumn. Most of the fish that moved downstream were age-2 or older, which is typical of bull trout in other areas. We do not know the extent or timing of emigrations of age-0 fish, an important omission from this study.

We do not know the contribution of different age classes and life history strategies to juvenile and adult production. Certainly, maintaining the expression of life history diversity, spread over multiple age classes, will help these fish survive temporal habitat disturbances. The contribution of various life history strategies expressed by juvenile bull trout could be evaluated, at least in part, by simply maintaining the current network of PIT tag interrogation systems. Much effort was expended to PIT tag juvenile bull trout, and those with successful life history strategies will mature and should be detectable by the interrogators used in this project for years to come, as well as by recapture when electrofishing or trapping. With a minimum of maintenance, PIT tag interrogators should be able to collect data documenting the timing of spawning migrations and periods when fluvial, adult fish use river and stream habitat. Because the PIT tag interrogation systems continued to operate in 2008 and 2009, additional information on fish movements was collected and more information will be available about the success of different juvenile life histories and from adult fish behavior and use of tributaries in the Jarbidge River basin. In addition, and of substantial ecological and management significance, the PTISs and the resultant data they provide will establish a baseline for monitoring changes in fish behavior in response to future environmental changes.

To document changes in the Jarbidge River bull trout population over time, we suggest a sampling regime that combines a broad comparison of relative fish abundance and distribution in several tributaries with a more detailed population estimate in one or more streams. For now, we suggest that a mark-recapture population estimate be conducted in Jack Creek every 3-5 years. We also suggest monitoring fish population trends via single-pass electrofishing in upper West Fork Jarbidge River, Pine Creek, and Dave Creek at regular intervals, such as every 3 to 5 years. These streams should be targeted based on their relative bull trout abundance and the ease of accessibility for field crews. We expect that as repeated measures become available, trends in population characteristics should become evident.

Acknowledgments

We want to acknowledge all the members of the Bull Trout Recovery Team, especially Selena Werdon and Allen Taylor of the USFWS, for their involvement, interaction, and funding support. We thank Steven Buschback, Emily Hite, Jason Olds, Dawn Hunt, Carrie Munz, and Brien Rose of United States Geological Survey's Columbia River Research Laboratory for working tireless hours in the field. We thank Kate Forster, Daniel Armichardy, Jessica Stegmeier, Matthew Kowalski, and Josh Uriarte from the Bureau of Land Management in Twin Falls for their placement of thermographs, collection of water temperature data, and assistance in fish sampling and maintaining and downloading the PIT tag interrogation systems. We also thank the personnel at the United States Forest Service, Wells District Ranger Station for use of the Mahoney facility for housing and equipment storage. Krinn and Chuck McCoy of the Tshawhawbitts Bed and Breakfast hosted the field crew and provided information on the area. We would like to recognize Gary Johnson and Caleb Cotton of Nevada Department of Wildlife for their help maintaining the PIT tag interrogation systems. We appreciate the many volunteers for the pack trips and the horse pack leaders in 2006 and 2007. We thank Kenney Baird for allowing us to store equipment on his property; and we thank the citizens of Jarbidge, Nevada, for their patience and many interesting conversations.

References

Anderson, C.S., 1985, The structure of sculpin populations along a stream size gradient: Environmental Biology of Fishes v. 13, p. 93-102.

Bain, M.B., and Stevenson, N.J., 1999, Aquatic habitat assessment—Common methods: American Fisheries Society, Bethesda, Md., p. 149-155.

Beauchamp, D.A., and Van Tassell, J.J., 2001, Modeling seasonal trophic interactions of adfluvial bull trout in Lake Billy Chinook, Oregon: Transactions of the American Fisheries Society, v. 130, p. 204-216.

Bellerud, B.L., Gunkel, S., Hemmingsen, A.R., Buchannan, D.V., and Howell, P.J., 1997, Bull trout life history, genetics, habitat needs, and limiting factors in central and northeast Oregon, Annual Report to the Bonneville Power Administration, Project 95-64, Portland, Oreg.

Bisson, P.A., Montgomery, D.R., and Buffington, J.M., 2006, Valley segments, stream reaches, and channel units, pg. 23-49 *in* Hauer, F.R., and Lamberti, G.A., eds., Methods in stream ecology: Academic Press, Burlington, Mass.

Brenkman, S.J., Corbett, S.C., and Volk, E.C., 2007, Use of otolith chemistry and radiotelemetry to determine age specific migratory patterns of anadromous bull trout in the Hoh River, Washington: Transactions of the American Fisheries Society, v. 136, p. 1-11.

Connolly, P.J., Jezorek, I.G., Martens, K., and Prentice, E.F., 2008, Measuring performance of two stationary interrogation systems for detecting downstream and upstream movement of PIT-tagged salmonids: North American Journal of Fisheries Management, v. 28, p. 402-417.

Connolly, P.J., Jezorek, I.G., and Prentice, E.F., 2005, Development and use of in-stream PIT-tag detection systems to assess movement behavior of fish in tributaries of the Columbia River Basin, USA, p. 217-220 *in* Noldus, L.P. J., Grieco, F., Loijens, L.W.S., and Zimmerman, P.H., eds.: Proceedings of the Measuring Behavior 2005, 5th International Conference on Methods and Techniques in Behavioral Research. Noldus Information Technology, Wageningen,The Netherlands.

DeHaan, P., Ardren, W., Gilmore, T., and Werdon, S., 2007, Genetic Analysis of Bull Trout in the Jarbidge River Watershed, Nevada/Idaho draft report: Abernathy Fish Technology Center, Conservation Genetics Program.

Dieterman, D.J., and Hoxmeier, R.J., 2009, Instream evaluation of passive integrated transponder retention in brook trout and brown trout—Effects of season, anatomical placement, and fish length: North American Journal of Fisheries Management, v. 29, p. 109-115.

Donald, D.B., and Alger, D.J., 1993, Geographic distribution, species displacement, and niche Overlap or lake trout and bull trout in mountain lakes: Canadian Journal of Zoology, v. 71, p. 238-247.

Downs, C.C., Horan, D., Morgan-Harris, E., and Jakubowski, R., 2006, Spawning demographics and juvenile dispersal of an adfluvial bull trout population in Trestle Creek, Idaho: North American Journal of Fisheries Management, v. 26, p. 190-200.

Dunham, J.B., and Rieman, B.E., 1999, Metapopulation structure of bull trout: influences of physical, biotic, and geometrical landscape characteristics: Ecological Applications, v. 9, p. 642–655.

Dunham, J.B., Rieman, B.E., and Chandler, G.L., 2003a, Influences of temperature and environmental variables on the distribution of bull trout at the southern margin of its range: North American Journal of Fisheries Management, v. 23, p. 894–904.

Dunham, J.B., Schroeter, R.E., and Rieman, B.E., 2003b, Influence of maximum water temperature on occurrence of Lahontan cutthroat trout within streams: North American Journal of Fisheries Management, v. 23, p. 1042–1049.

Elton, C.S., 1958, The ecology of invasion: John Wiley Sons, New York.

Fraley, J.J., and Shepard, B.B., 1989, Life history, ecology and population status of migratory bull trout (*Salvelinus confluentus*) in the Flathead Lake and River system: Montana: Northwest Science, v. 63, p. 133-143.

Johnson, G., 2002, Jack Creek bull trout inventory, *in* Johnson, G., Statewide fisheries management Federal Aid job progress reports F-20-37: Native fishes/amphibian management, Eastern Region, Nevada Division of Wildlife, Elko, Nevada.

Haas, G.R., and McPhail, J.D., 2001, The post-Wisconsinian glacial biogeography of bull trout (*Salvelinus confluentus*)—A multivariate morphometric approach for conservation biology and management: Canadian Journal of Fisheries and Aquatic Science, v. 58, p. 2189-2203.

Harvey, B.C., White., J.L., and Nakamoto R.J., 2004, An emergent multiple predator effect may enhance biotic resistance in a stream fish assemblage: Ecology, v. 85, p. 127-133.

Hawkins, C.P., Kershner, J.L., Bisson, P.A., Bryant, M.D., Decher, L.M., Gregory, S.V., McCullough, D.A., Overton, C.K., Reeves, G.H., Steedman, R.J., and Young, M.K., 1993, A hierarchical approach to classifying stream habitat features: Fisheries, v. 18, p. 3-12.

Homel, K., and Budy, P., 2008, Temporal and spatial variability in the migration patterns of juvenile and subadult bull trout in Northeastern Oregon: Transactions of the American Fisheries Society, v. 137, p. 869-880.

Hughes, N.F., 1998, A model of habitat selection by drift-feeding stream salmonids at different scales: Ecology, v. 79, p. 281-294.

McPhail, J.D., and Murray, C.B., 1979, The early life history and ecology of Dolly Varden (*Salvelinus malma*) in the upper Arrow Lakes: Unpublished report to the British Columbia Hydro and Power Authority and the Fish and Wildlife Branch, Kootenay Region, Cranbrook, British Columbia.

Mesa, M.G., Weiland, L.K., and Zydlewski, G.B., 2004, Critical swimming speeds of wild bull trout: Northwest Science, v. 78, p. 59-65.

Mogen, J.T., and Kaeding, L.R., 2005, Identification and characterization of migratory and nonmigratory bull trout populations in the St. Mary River drainage, Montana: Transactions of the American Fisheries Society, v. 135, p. 841-852

Monnot, L., Dunham, J.B., Hoem, T., and Koetsier P., 2008, Influences of body size and environment factors on autumn downstream migration of bull trout in the Boise River, Idaho: North American Journal of Fisheries Management, v. 28, p. 231-240.

Muhlfeld, C.C., Glutting, S., Hunt, R., Daniels, D., and Marotz, B., 2003, Winter diel habitat use and movement by subadult bull trout in the upper Flathead River, Montana: North American Journal of Fisheries Management, v. 23, p. 163-171.

Muhlfeld, C.C., and Marotz, B., 2005, Seasonal movement and habitat use by subadult bull trout in the upper Flathead River system: North American Journal of Fisheries Management, v. 25, p. 797-810.

Patrick, R., 1975, Structure of stream communities, *in* Cody, M.L., and Diamond, J.M., eds.: Ecology and evolution of communities: The Belknap Press of Harvard University Press, Cambridge, Mass., p.445-459

Paul, A.J., and Post, J.R., 2001, Spatial distribution of native and nonnative salmonids in streams of the eastern slopes of the Canadian Rocky Mountains: Transactions of the American Fisheries Society, v. 130, p. 417–430.

Ratliff, D.E., 1992, Bull trout investigations in the Metolius River-Lake Billy Chinook System, *in* Howell, P.J., and Buchanan, D.V., eds., Proceedings of the Gearhart Mountain Bull Trout Workshop: American Fisheries Society, Oregon Chapter, Corvallis, Oreg., p. 37-44.

Reynolds, J.B., 1983, Electrofishing, *in* Nielson, L.A., and Johnson, D.L., eds., Fisheries techniques: American Fisheries Society, Bethesda, Md., p. 147-163

Rieman, B.E., and McIntyre, J.D., 1993, Demographic and habitat requirements for conservation of bull trout: U.S. Forest Service General Technical Report INT-308.

Rieman, B.E., Isaak, D., Adams, S., Horan, D., Nagel, D., Luce, C., and Myers D., 2007, Anticipated climate warming effects on bull trout habitats and populations across the interior Columbia River basin: Transactions of the American Fisheries Society, v. 136, p. 1552-1567.

Ripley, T., Scrimgeour, G., and Boyce, M.S., 2005, Bull trout occurrence and abundance influenced by cumulative industrial developments in a Canadian boreal forest watershed: Canadian Journal of Fisheries and Aquatic Sciences, v. 62, p. 2431-2442.

Schlosser, I.J., 1982, Fish community structure and function along two habitat gradients in a headwater stream: Ecological Monographs, v. 52, p. 395-414.

Seber, G.A.F., 1982, The estimation of animal abundance and related parameters, 2nd ed.: Macmillan Publishing Company, Inc. New York.

Stelfox, J.D., 1997, Seasonal movements, growth, survival and population status of the adfluvial bull trout population in lower Kananaskis Lake, Alberta, *in* Mackay, W.C., Brewin, M.K., and Monita, M., eds., Friends of the Bull Trout conference Proceedings: Bull Trout Task Force (Alberta), c/o Trout Unlimited Canada, Calgary, p. 309-316

Swanberg, T., 1997, Movements of and habitat use of fluvial bull trout in the Blackfoot River, Montana: Transactions of the American Fisheries Society, v. 126, p. 735-746.

U.S. Fish and Wildlife Service, 2004, Draft Recovery Plan for the Jarbidge River Distinct Population Segment of Bull Trout (*Salvelinus confluentus*): U.S. Fish and Wildlife Service, Portland, Oreg.

Ward, D.M., Winslow, K.H., and Folt, C.L., 2008, Do native species limit survival of reintroduced Atlantic salmon in historic rearing streams?: Biological Conservation, v. 141, p. 146-152.

Zalewski, M., and Cowx, I.G., 1990, Factors affecting the efficiency of electric fishing, *in* Cowx and Lamarque, P., eds., Fishing with electricity: Fishing News Books, Oxford, UK., p. 89-110.

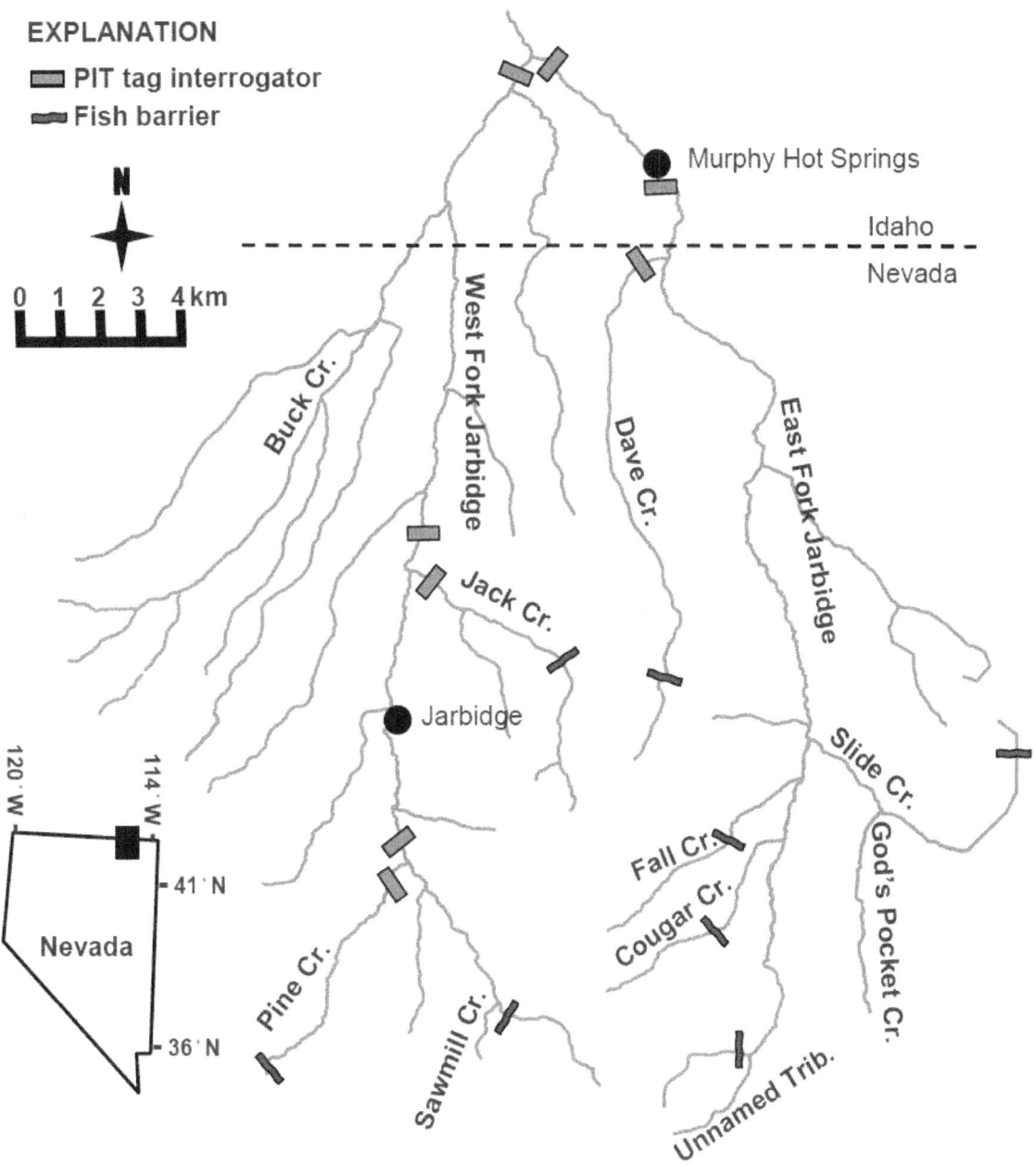

Figure 1. Map of the East and West Forks of the Jarbidge River, Idaho and Nevada, with the locations of reported fish barriers and passive integrated transponder (PIT) tag interrogations systems installed in 2006 or 2007.

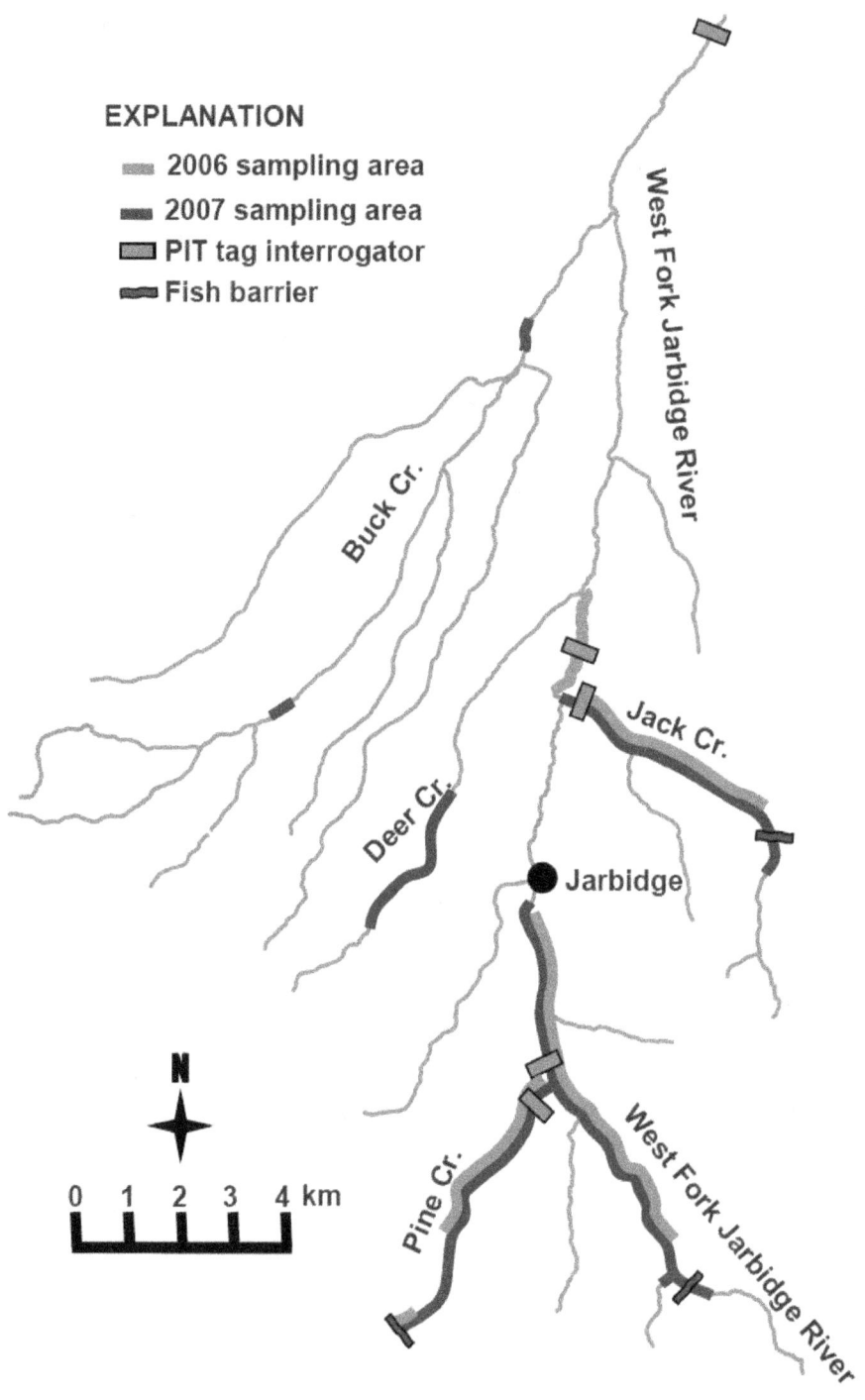

Figure 2. Locations of fish and habitat surveys, fish barriers, and passive integrated transponder (PIT) tag interrogation systems in the West Fork Jarbidge River, Nevada, and its tributaries, 2006 and 2007. The interrogation systems at the confluence of Pine Creek and West Fork Jarbidge River, Nevada, and at the confluence of the East Fork and West Fork Jarbidge River, Idaho, were not installed until 2007.

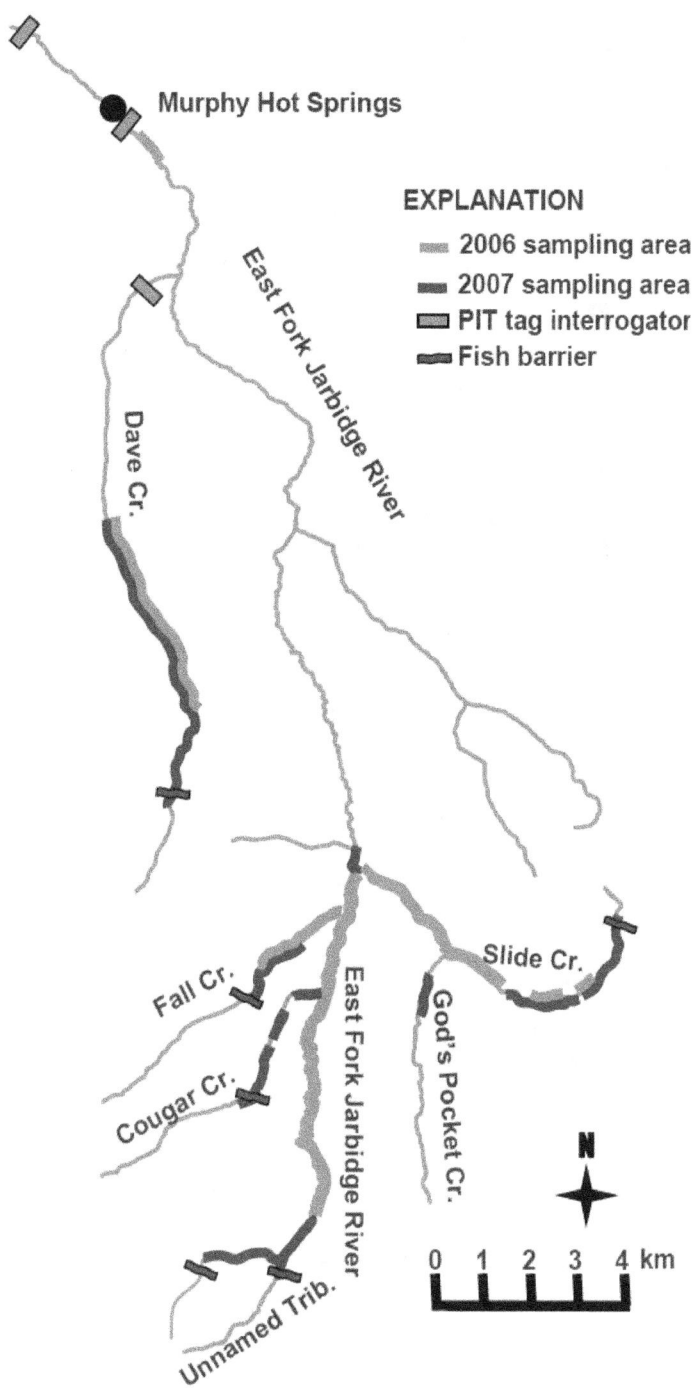

Figure 3. Locations of fish and habitat surveys, fish barriers, and passive integrated transponder (PIT) tag interrogation systems in the East Fork Jarbidge River, Nevada, and its tributaries, 2006 and 2007. The interrogation systems on Dave Creek, Nevada, and at the confluence of the East Fork and West Fork Jarbidge River, Idaho, were not installed until 2007.

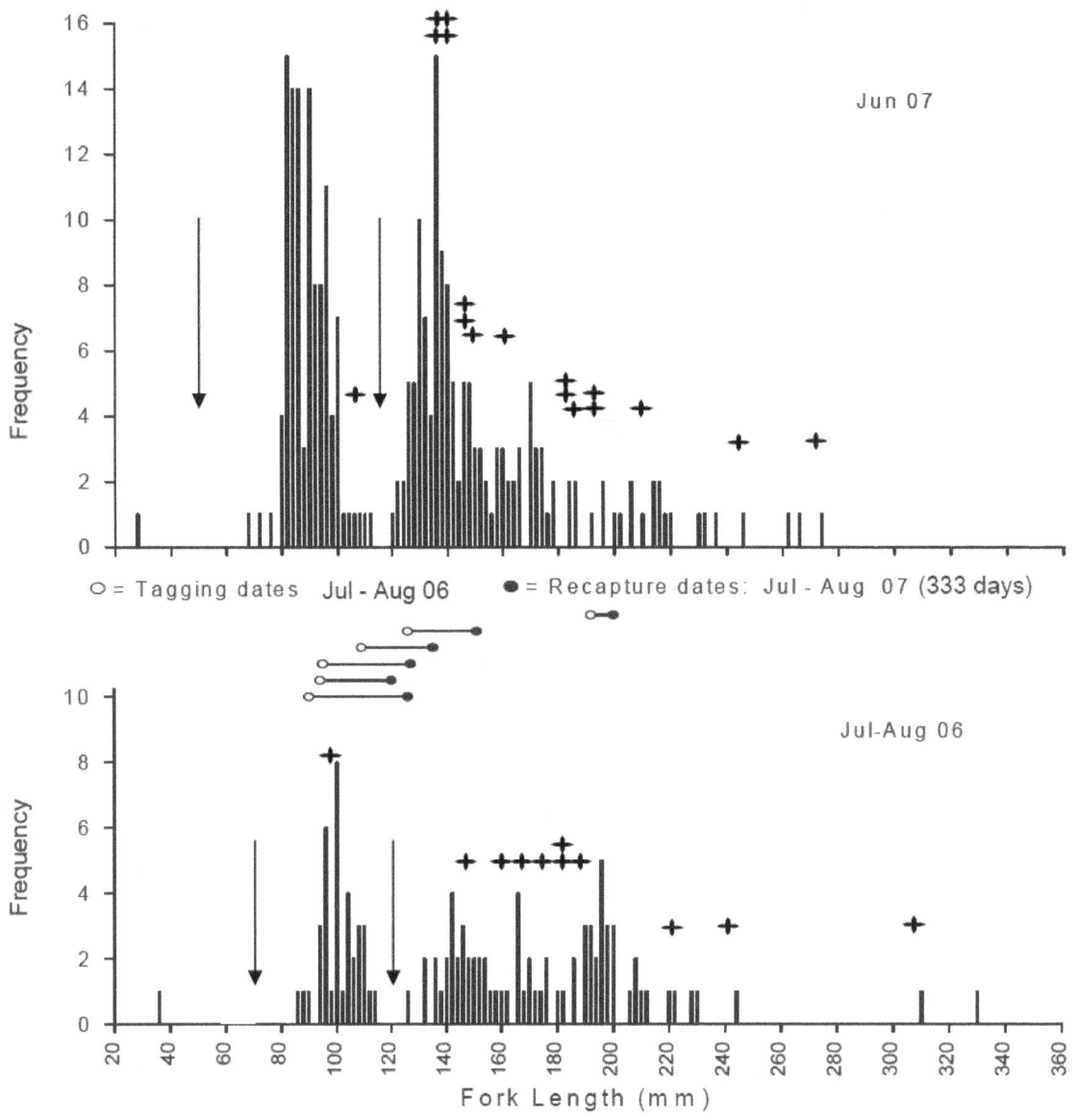

Figure 4. Length frequency, in 2-mm increments, of all bull trout sampled in the West Fork Jarbidge River, Nevada, in 2006 and 2007. The horizontal lines indicate the growth of individual fish that were tagged in 2006 and recaptured in 2007. The median number of days between tagging and recapture are shown in parentheses. Sampling effort is not the same for each year. The symbol "+" indicates the fork length of fish at tagging that were detected at an interrogation site after tagging. Vertical arrows indicate the break between age-0, age-1, and age-2 or older bull trout.

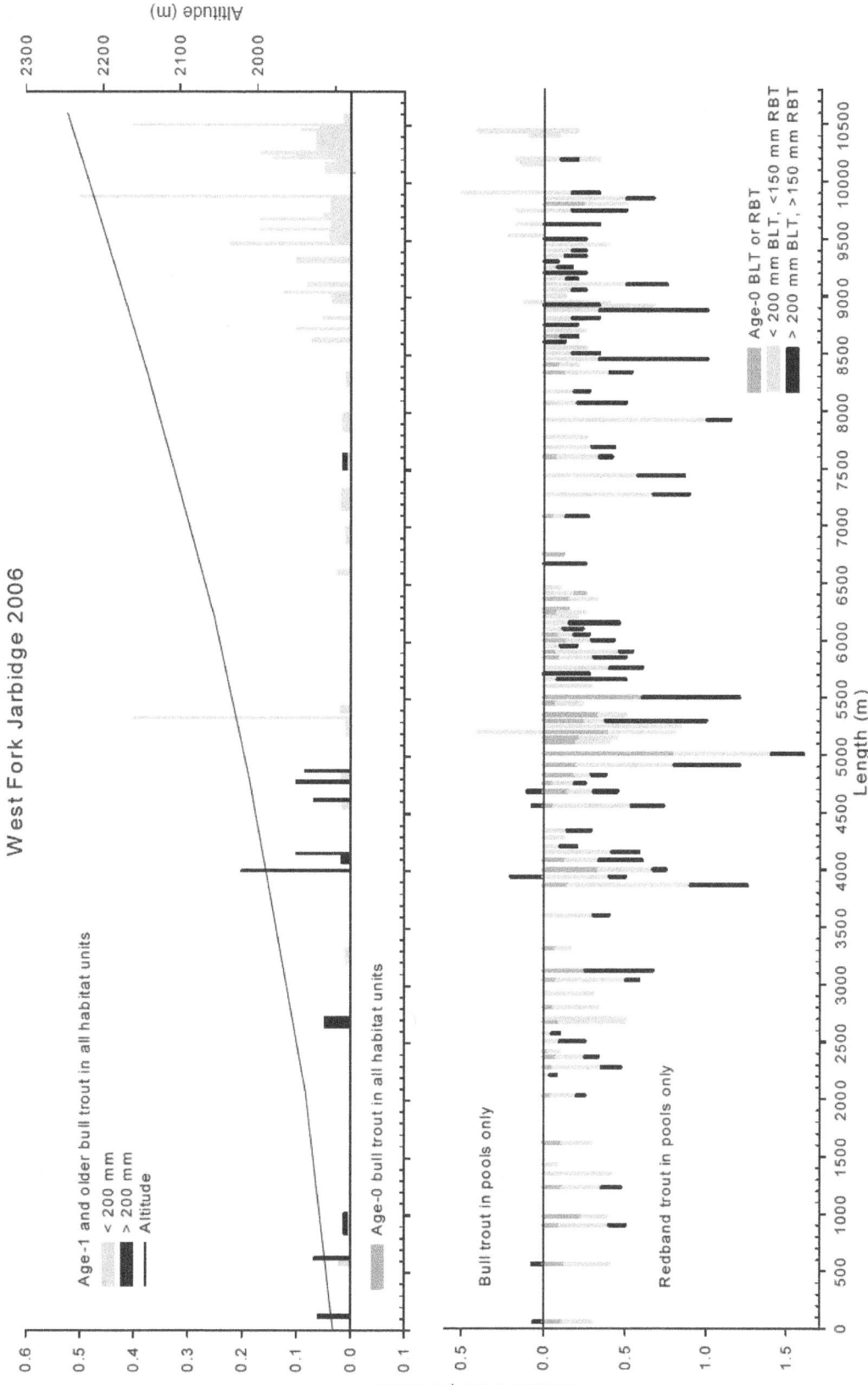

Figure 5. Number of bull trout (BLT) per meter by size class for all habitat units sampled along with altitude (upper graph) and the number of bull trout and redband trout (RBT) per meter by size class in pools only (lower graph) in West Fork Jarbidge River (rkm 21.5 – 30.2), Nevada, 2006.

29

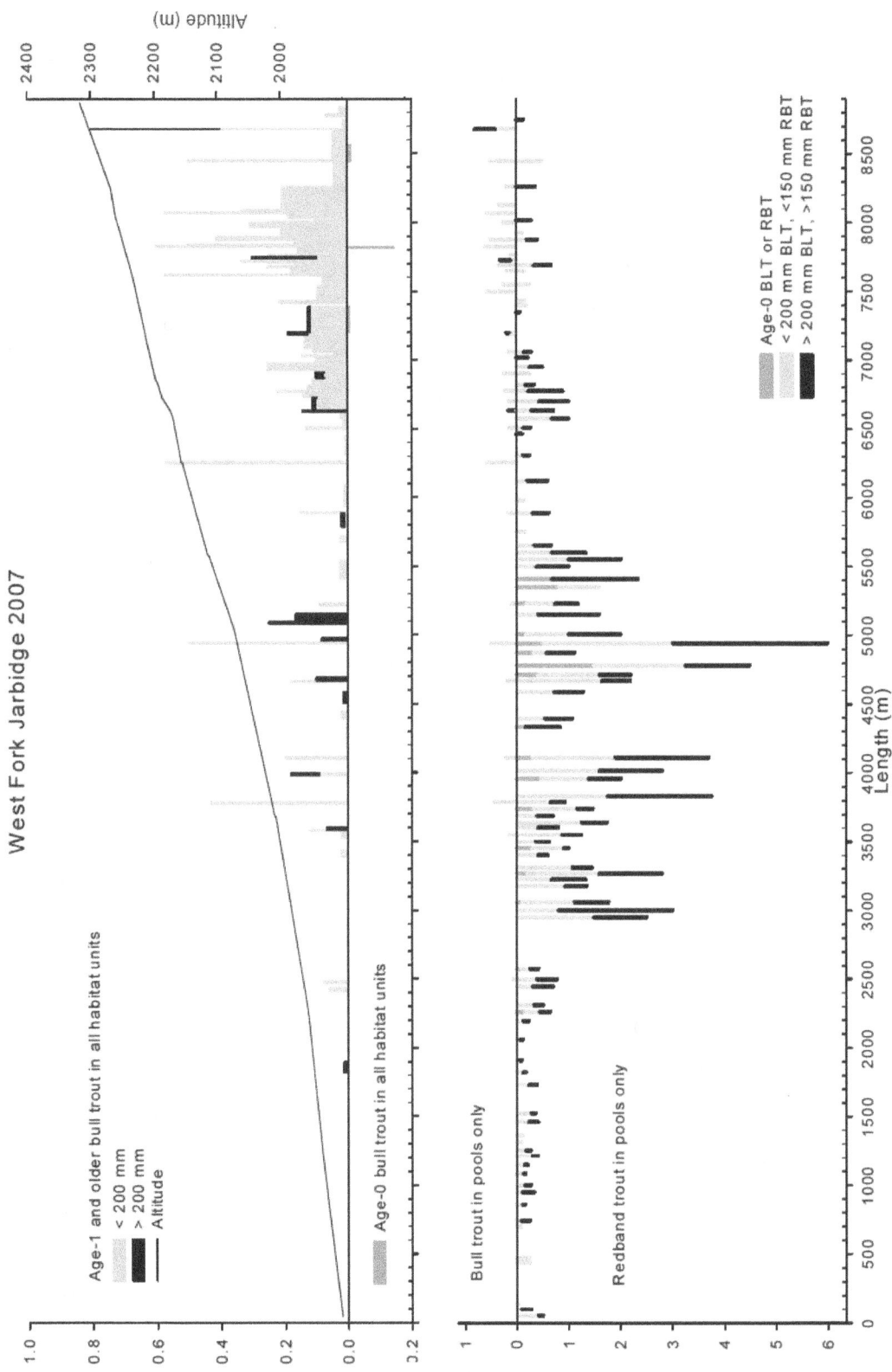

Figure 6. Number of bull trout (BLT) per meter by size class for all habitat units sampled along with altitude (upper graph) and the number of bull trout and redband trout (RBT) per meter by size class in pools only (lower graph) in West Fork Jarbidge River (rkm 21.7 – 32.2), Nevada, 2007.

30

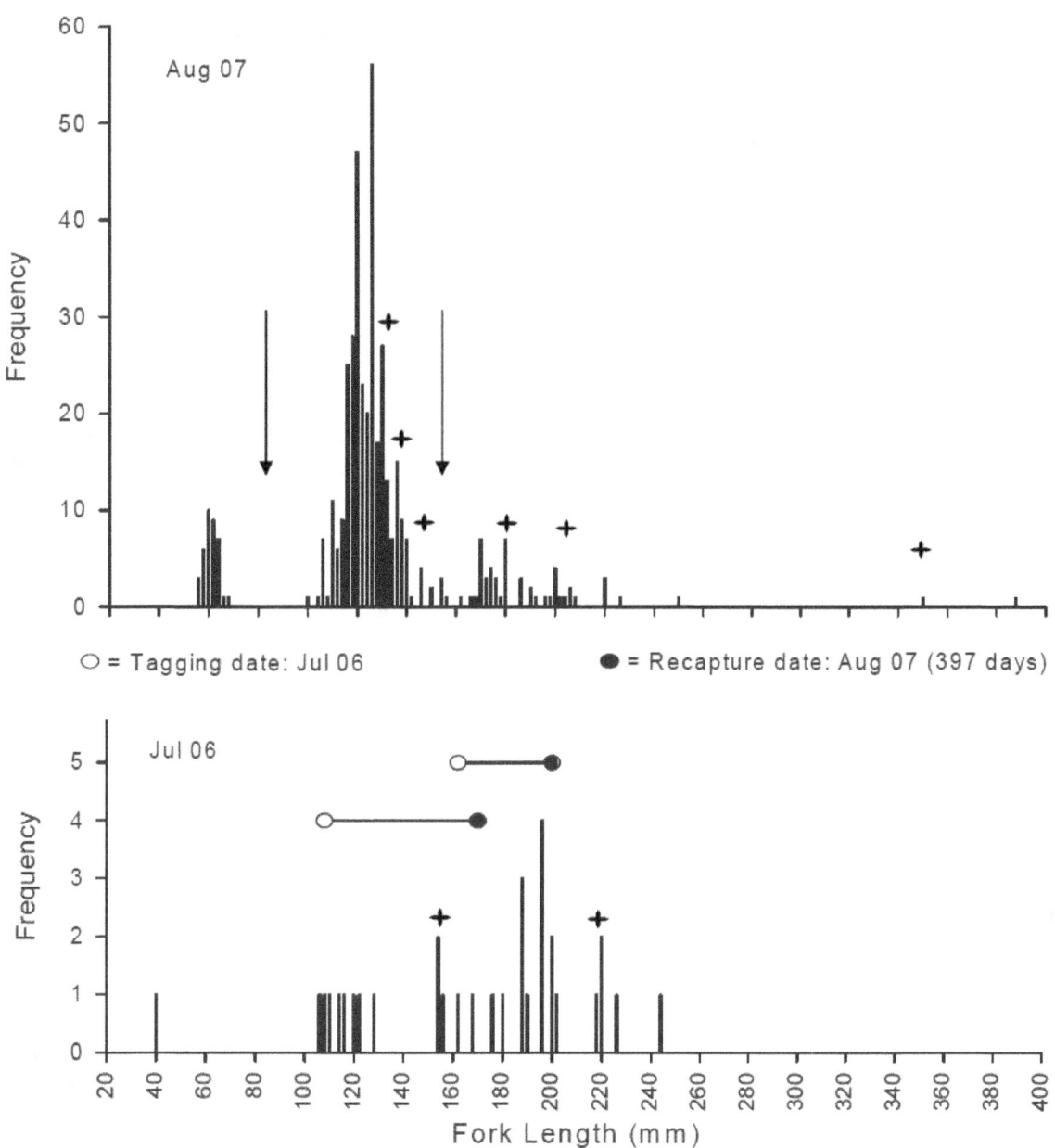

Figure 7. Length frequency ,in 2-mm increments, of all bull trout sampled in Pine Creek of the West Fork Jarbidge River subbasin, Nevada in 2006 and 2007. The horizontal lines indicate the growth of individual fish that were tagged in 2006 and recaptured in 2007. The mean number of days between tagging and recapture are shown in parentheses. The symbol "+" indicates the fork length of fish at tagging that were detected at an interrogation site after tagging. Vertical arrows indicate the break between age-0, age-1, or age-2 or older bull trout.

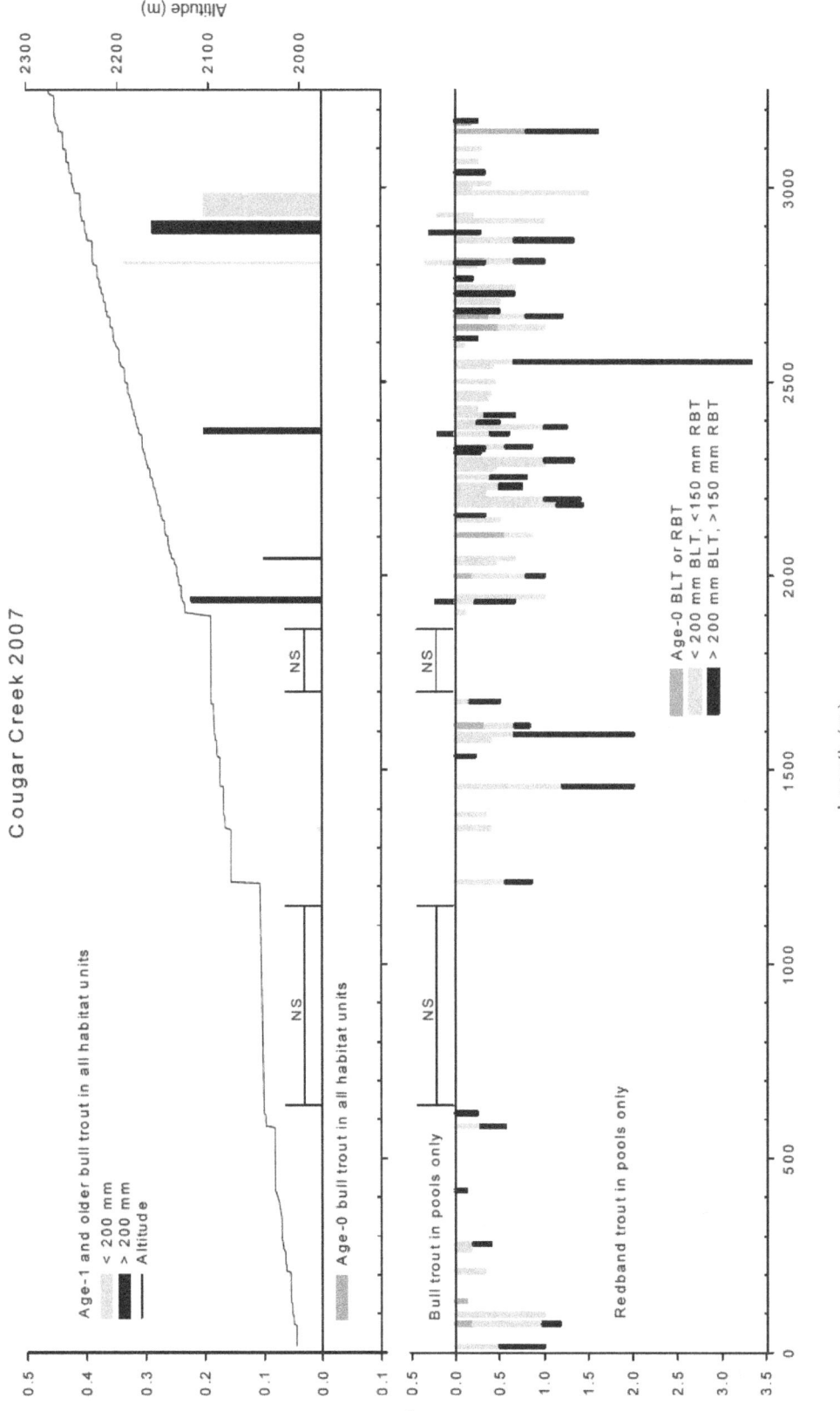

Figure 8. Number of bull trout (BLT) per meter by size class for all habitat units sampled along with altitude (upper graph) and the number of bull trout and redband trout (RBT) per meter by size class in pools only (lower graph) in Pine Creek (rkm 0 – 6.5), Nevada, 2006. NS = not sampled.

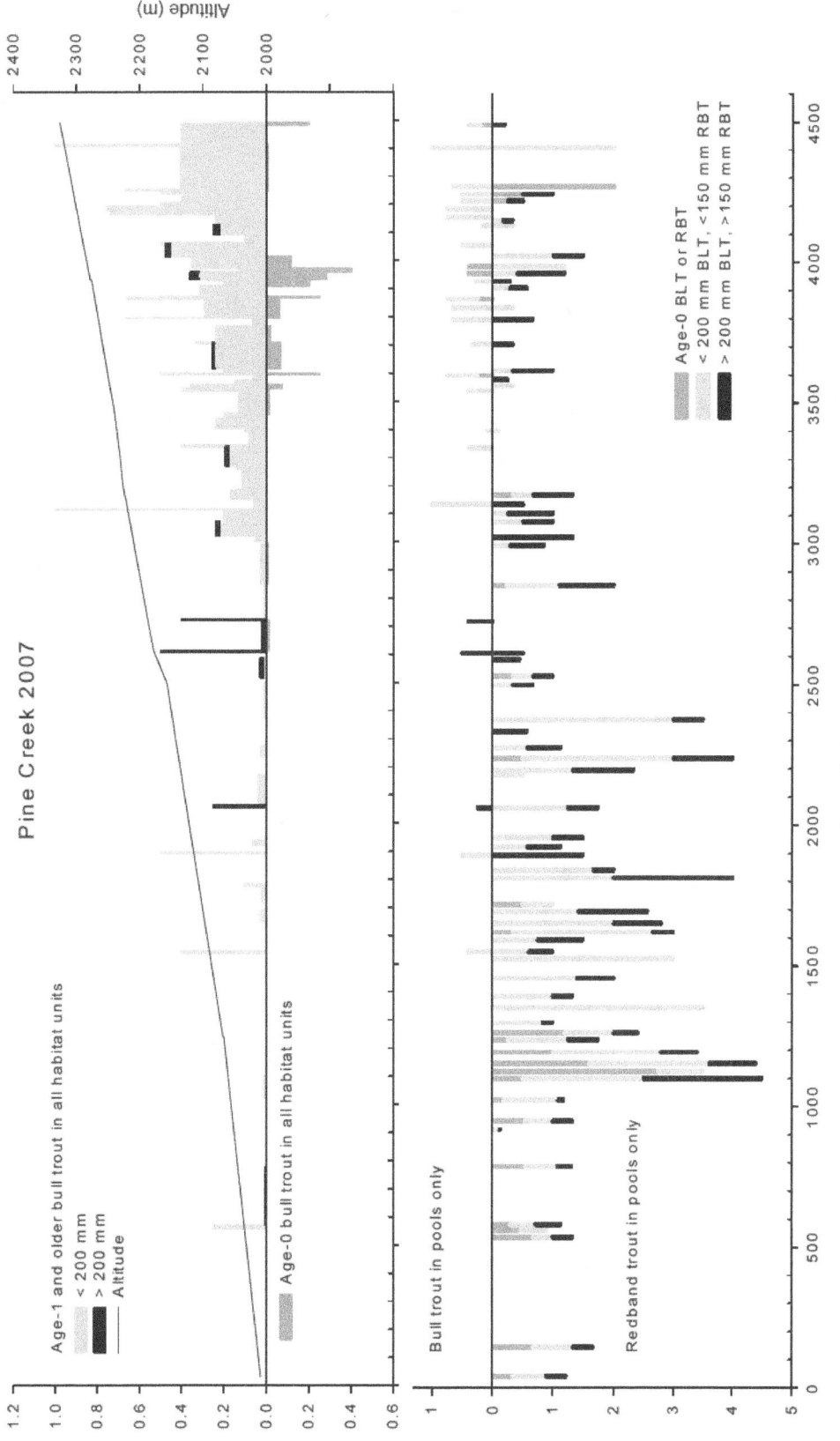

Figure 9. Number of bull trout (BLT) per meter by size class for all habitat units sampled along with altitude (upper graph) and the number of bull trout and redband trout (RBT) per meter by size class in pools only (lower graph) in Pine Creek (rkm 0 – 5.9), Nevada, 2007.

33

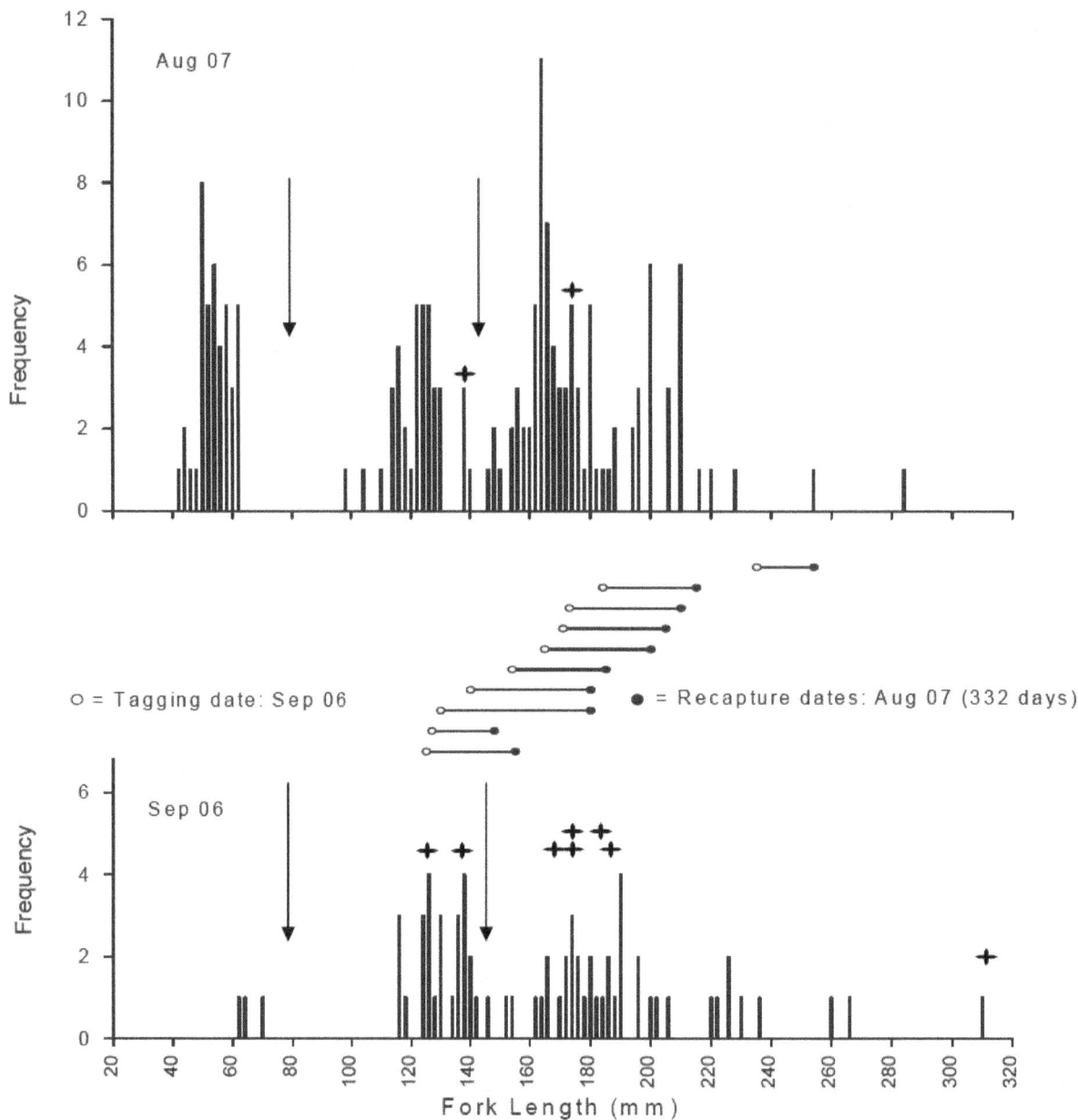

Figure 10. Length frequency in 2-mm increments of all bull trout sampled in Jack Creek of the West Fork Jarbidge River, Nevada, in 2006 and 2007. The horizontal lines indicate the growth of individual fish that were tagged in 2006 and recaptured in 2007. The number of days between tagging and recapture are shown in parentheses. The symbol "+" indicates the fork length of fish at tagging that were detected at an interrogation site after tagging. Vertical arrows indicate the break between age-0, age-1, and age-2 or older bull trout

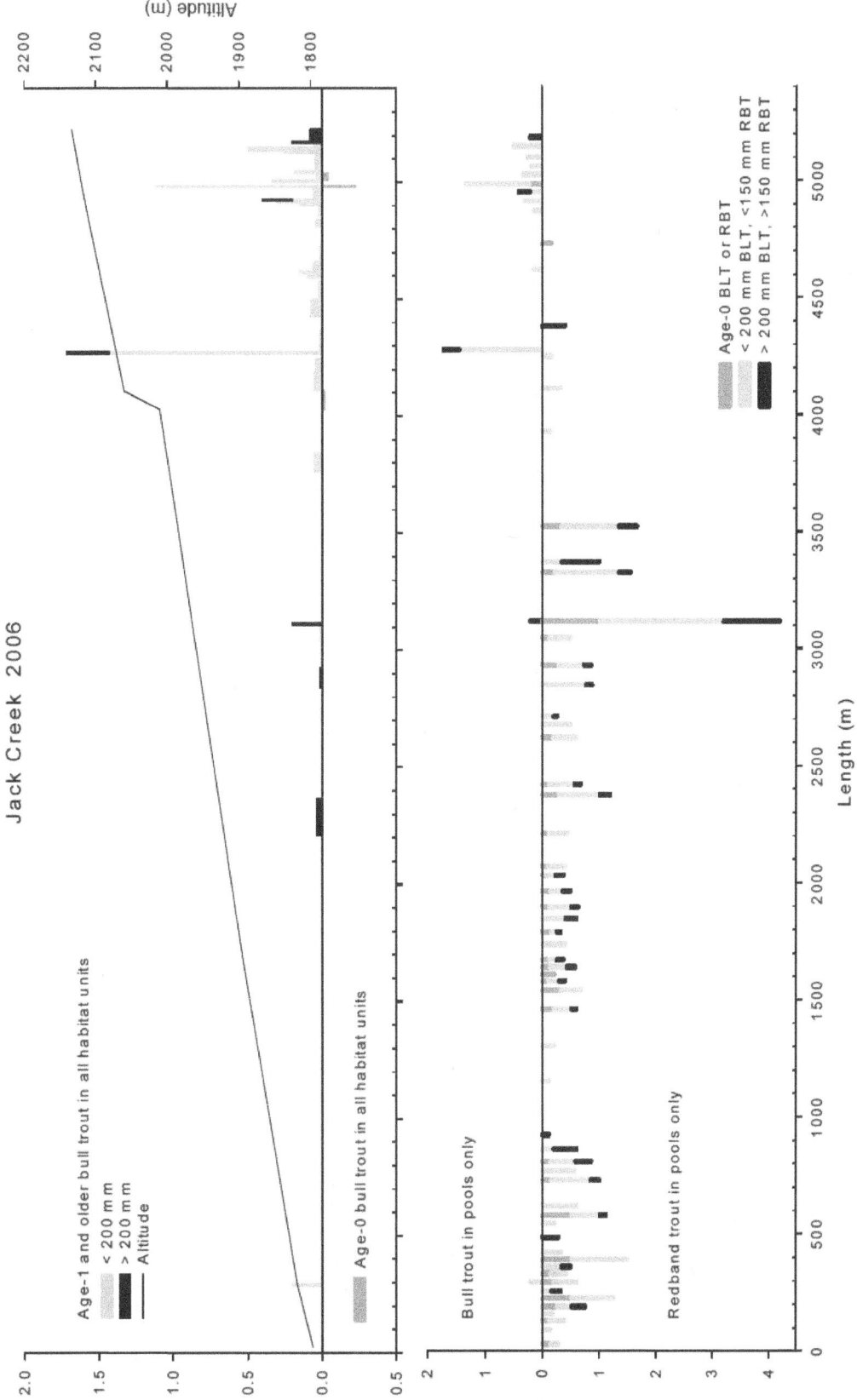

Figure 11. Number of bull trout (BLT) per meter by size class for all habitat units sampled along with altitude (upper graph) and the number of bull trout and redband trout (RBT) per meter by size class in pools only (lower graph) in Jack Creek (rkm 0 – 4.3), Nevada, 2006.

35

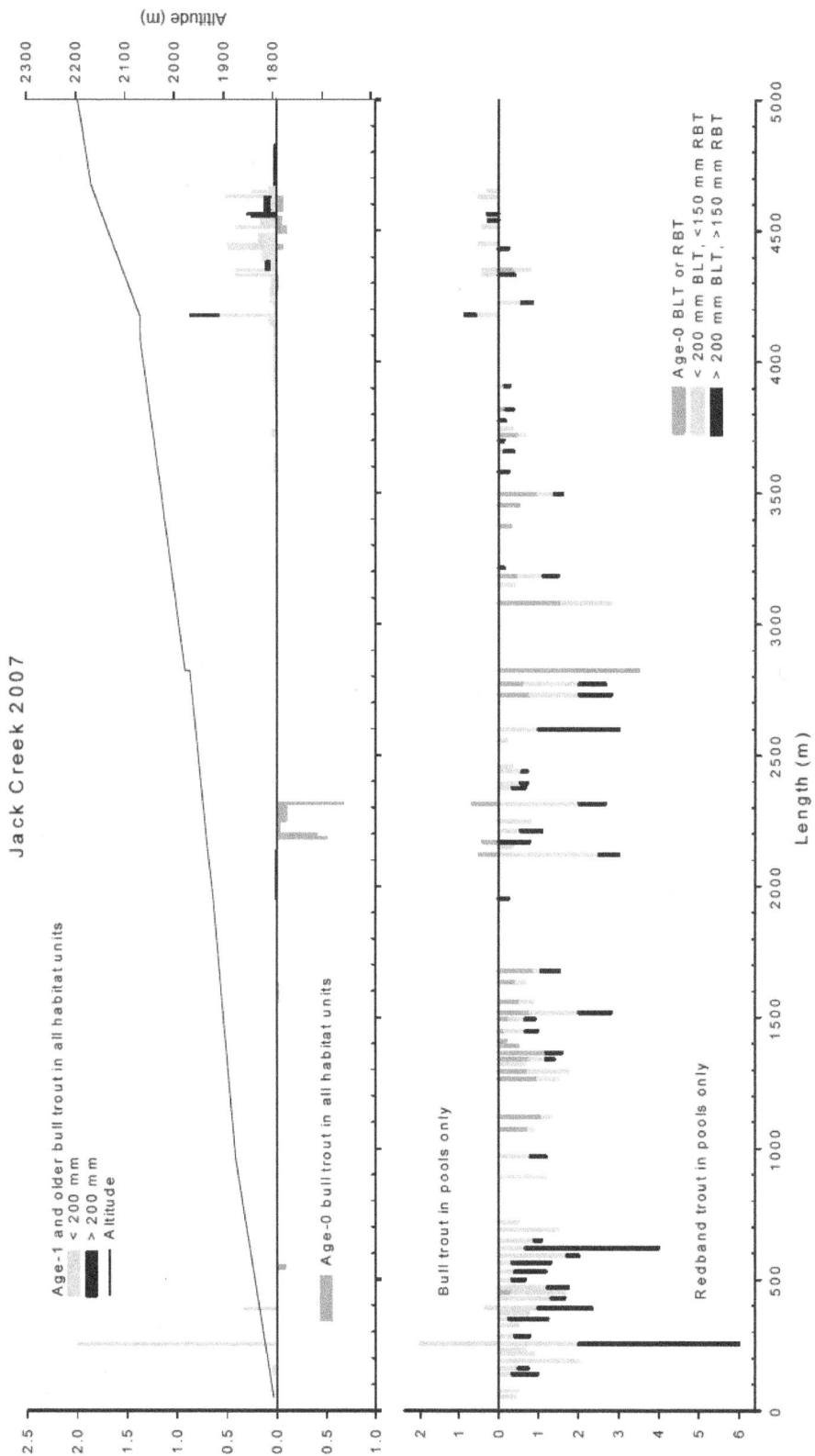

Figure 12. Number of bull trout (BLT) per meter, by size class, for all habitat units sampled along with altitude (upper graph) and the number of bull trout and redband trout (RBT) per meter by size class in pools only (lower graph) in Jack Creek (rkm 0 – 5.4), Nevada, 2007.

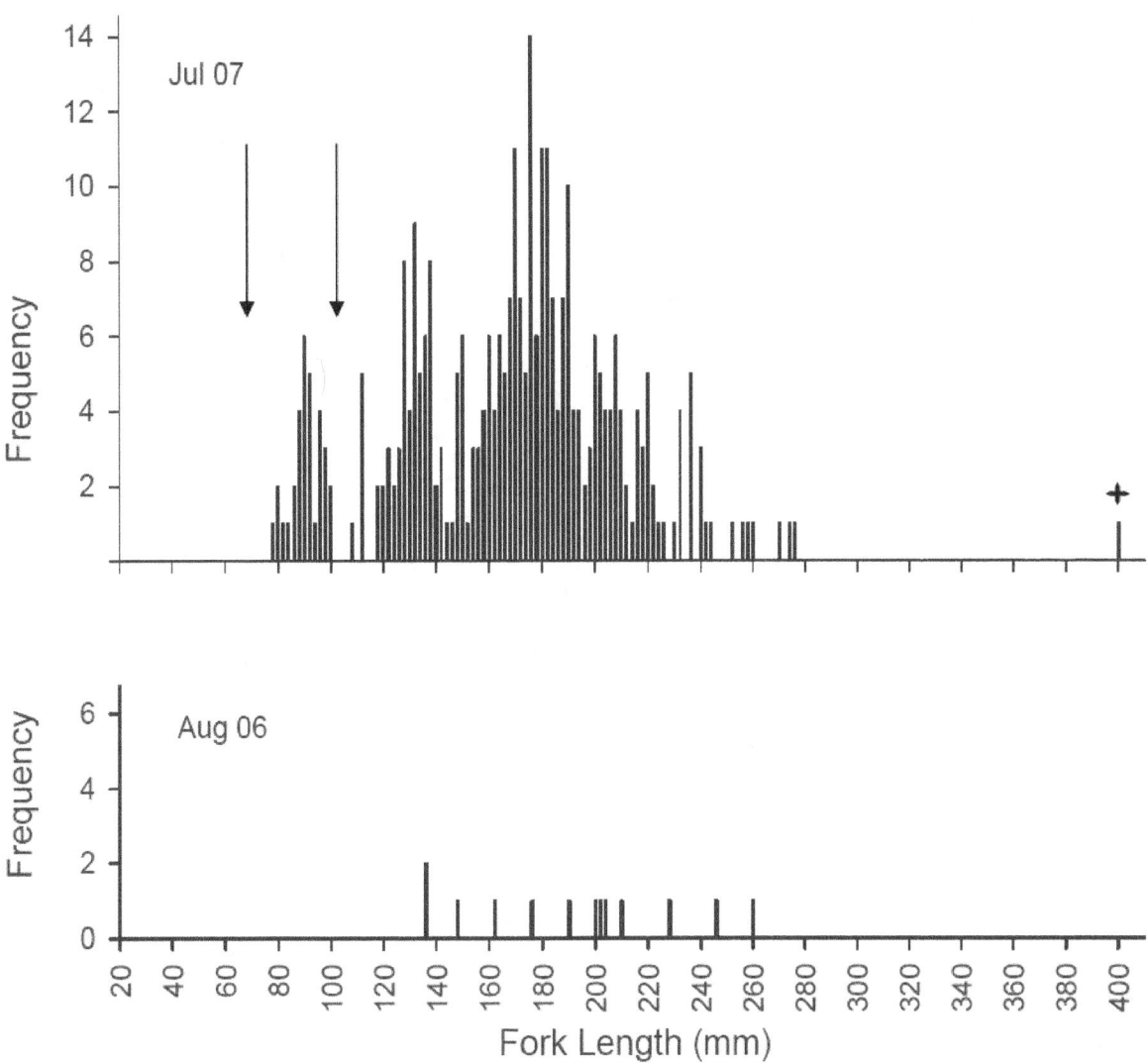

Figure 13. Length frequency in 2-mm increments of all bull trout sampled in the East Fork Jarbidge River, Nevada, in 2006 and 2007. Sampling effort is not the same for each year. Vertical arrows indicate the break between age-0, age-1, and age-2 or older bull trout. The symbol "+" indicates the fork length of a fish that was recaptured in the East Fork Jarbidge River after being tagged in Fall Creek in 2006.

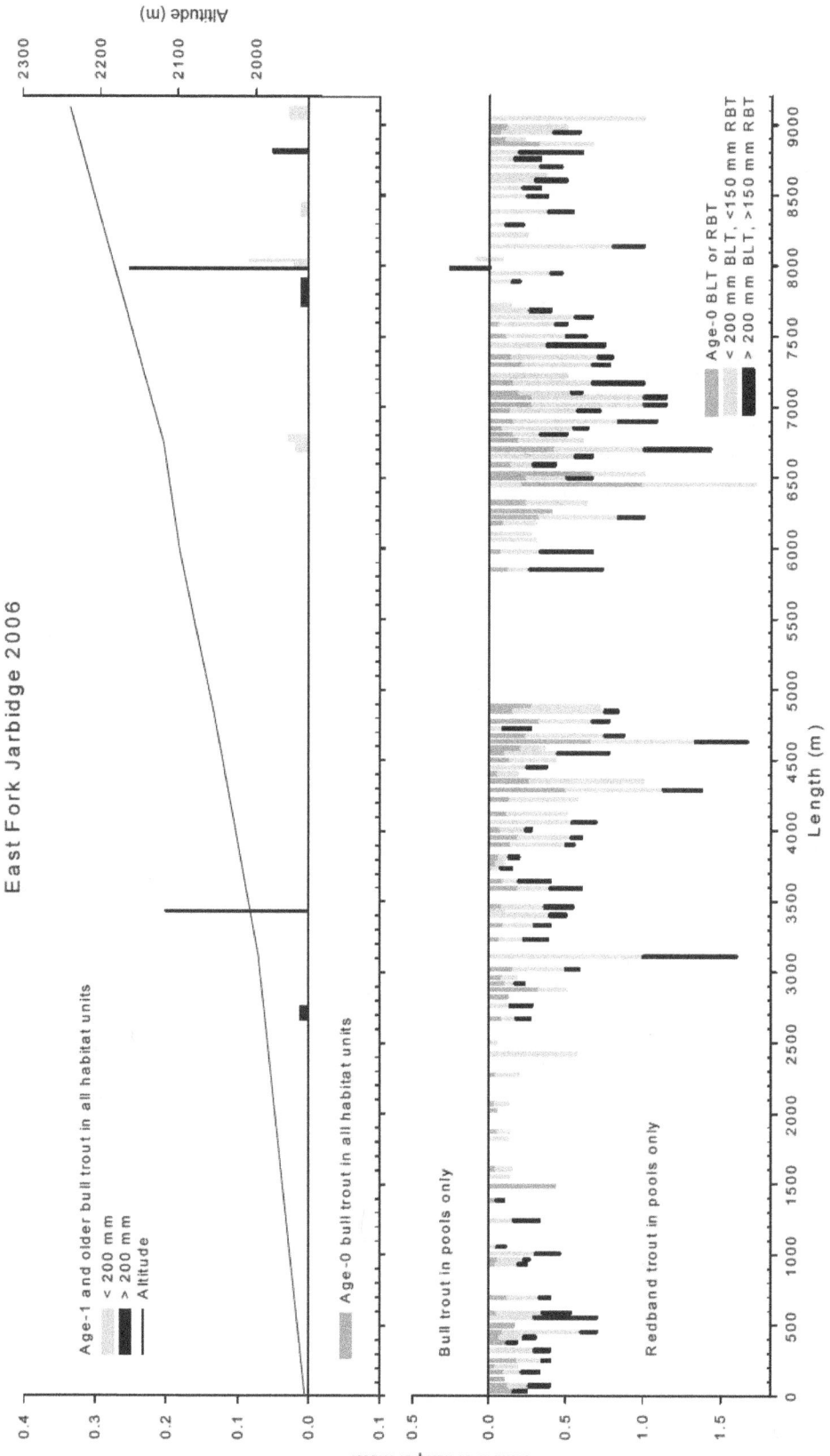

Figure 14. Number of bull trout (BLT) per meter by size class for all habitat units sampled along with altitude (upper graph) and the number of bull trout and redband trout (RBT) per meter by size class in pools only (lower graph) in East Fork Jarbidge River (rkm 15.6 – 24.7), Nevada, 2006. NS = not sampled.

38

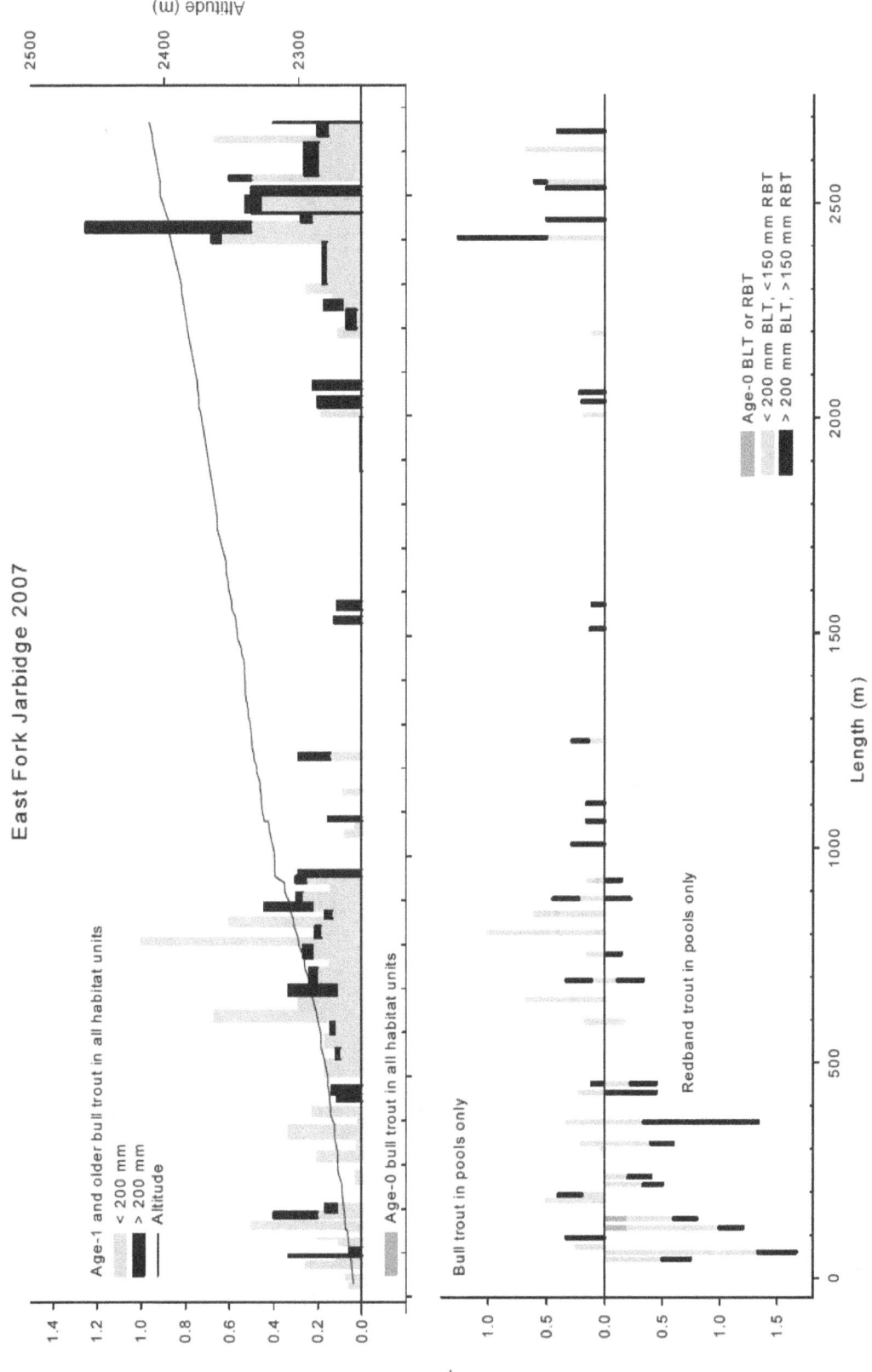

Figure 15. Number of bull trout (BLT) per meter by size class for all habitat units sampled along with altitude (upper graph) and the number of bull trout and redband trout (RBT) per meter by size class in pools only (lower graph) in East Fork Jarbidge River (rkm 32.5 – 35.0), Nevada, 2007.

39

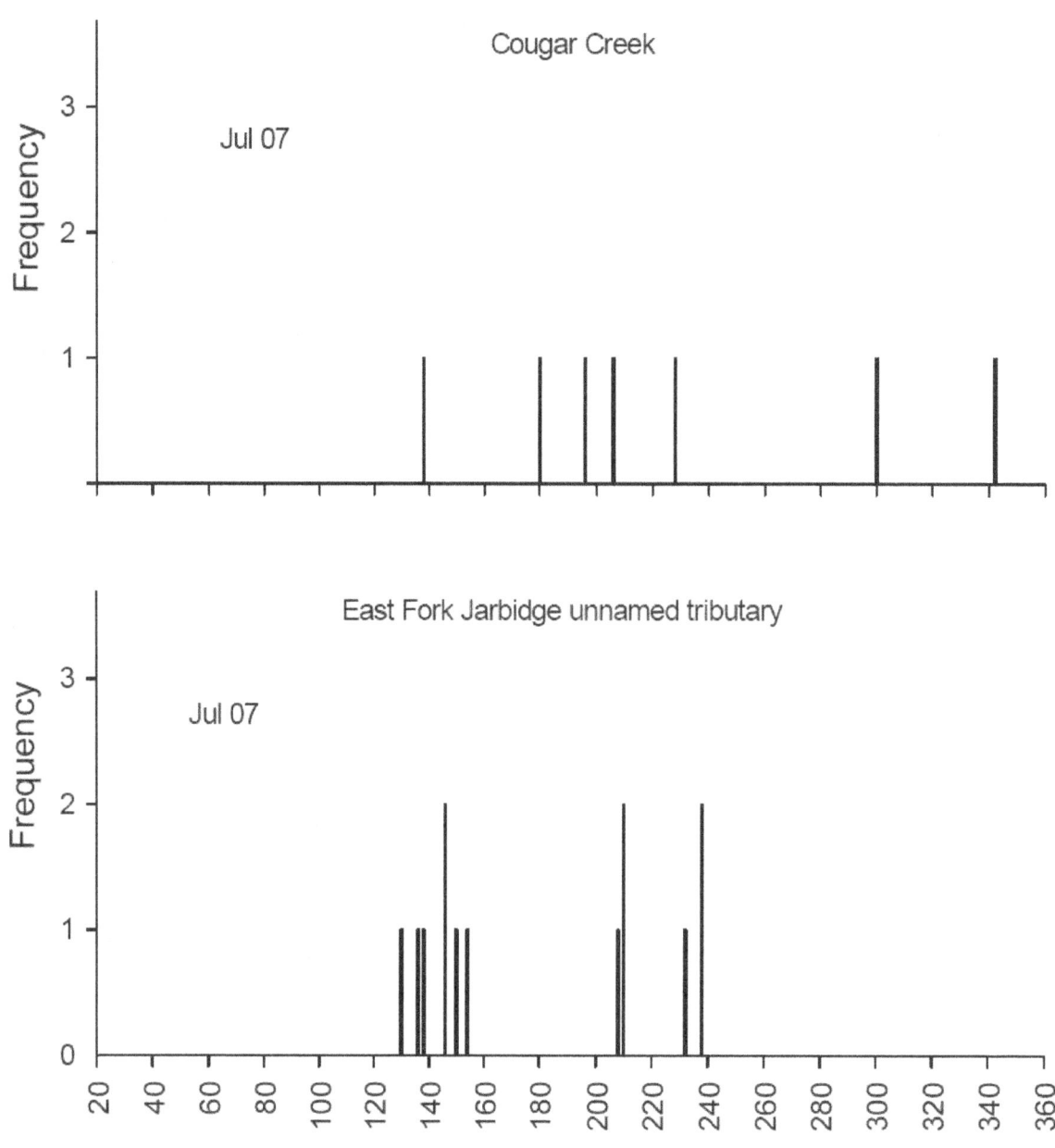

Figure 16. Length frequency in 2-mm increments of all bull trout sampled in Cougar Creek, Nevada, and an unnamed tributary of the East Fork Jarbidge River, Nevada, at rkm 33.5 (measured from the confluence with the West Fork Jarbidge River, Idaho), 2007.

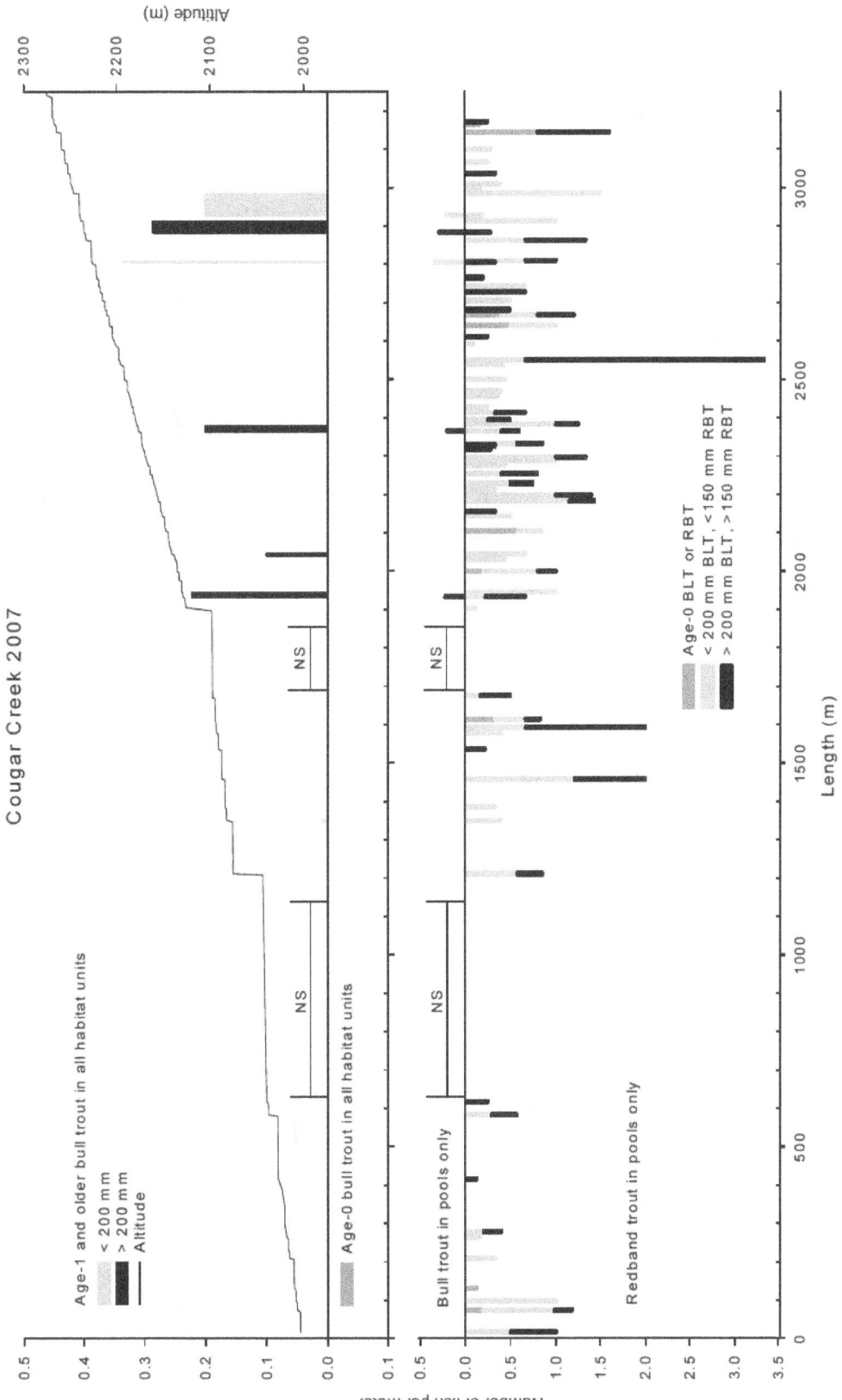

Figure 17. Number of bull trout (BLT) per meter by size class for all habitat units sampled along with altitude (upper graph) and the number of bull trout and redband trout (RBT) per meter by size class in pools only (lower graph) in Cougar Creek (rkm 0 – 3.1), Nevada, 2007. NS = not sampled.

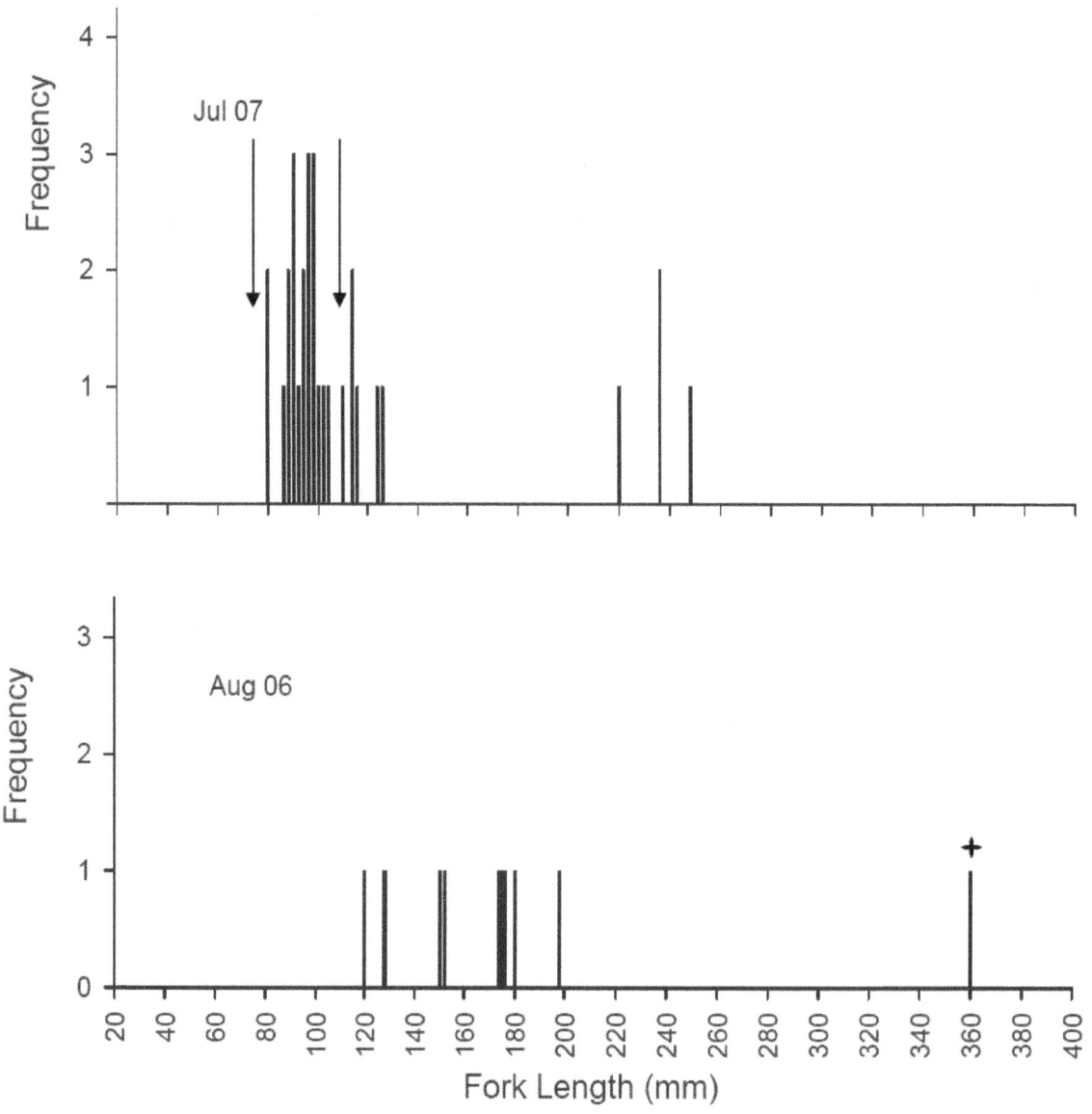

Figure 18. Length frequency in 2-mm increments of all bull trout sampled in Fall Creek of the East Fork Jarbidge River, Nevada, in 2006 and 2007. Sampling effort is not the same for each year. Vertical arrows indicate the break between age-0, age-1, and age-2 or older bull trout. The symbol "+" indicates the fork length of a fish that had moved and subsequently recaptured in the East Fork Jarbidge downstream of the confluence with Slide Creek.

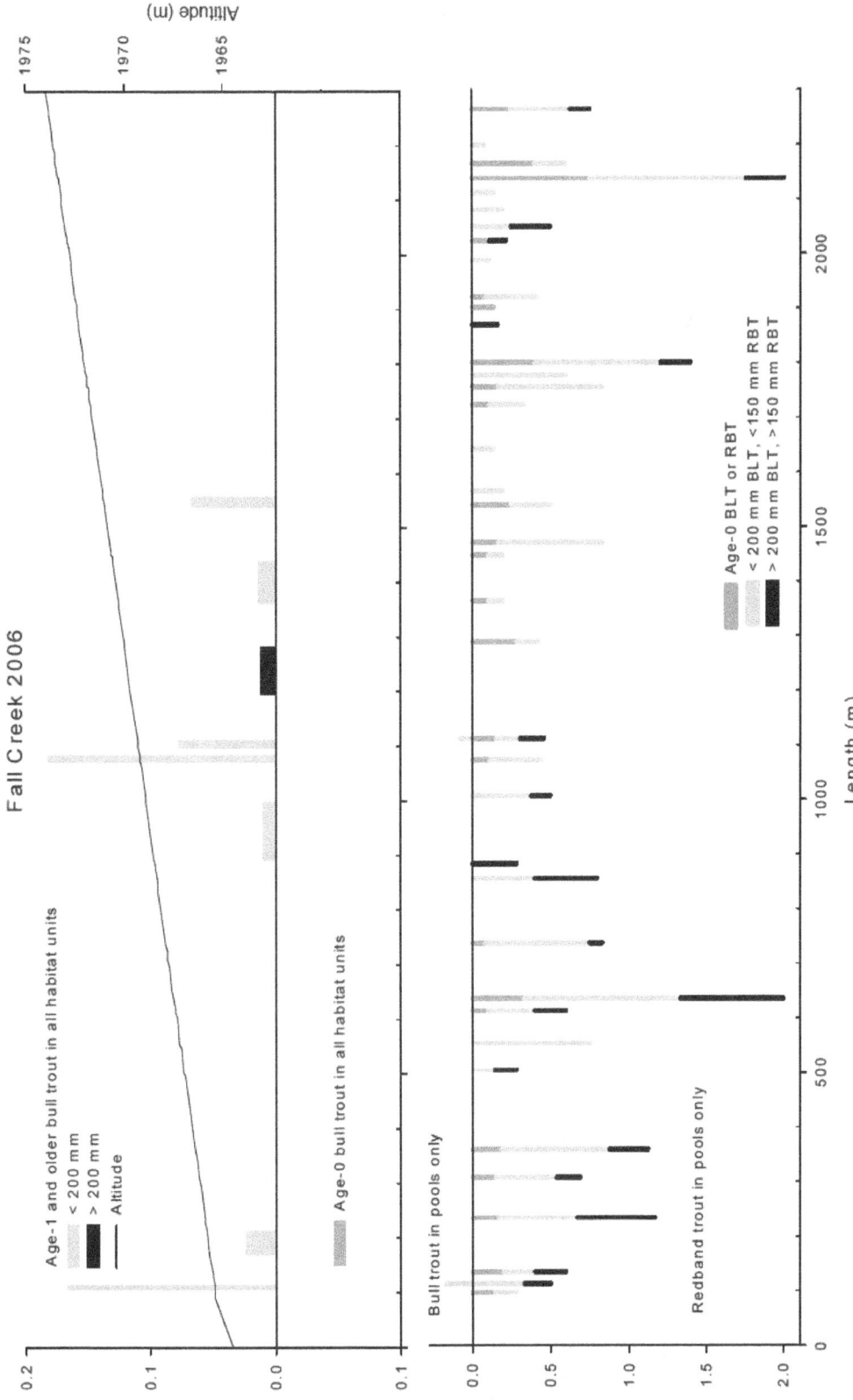

Figure 19. Number of bull trout (BLT) per meter by size class for all habitat units sampled along with altitude (upper graph) and the number of bull trout and redband trout (RBT) per meter by size class in pools only (lower graph) in Fall Creek (rkm 0 – 2.0), Nevada, 2006.

43

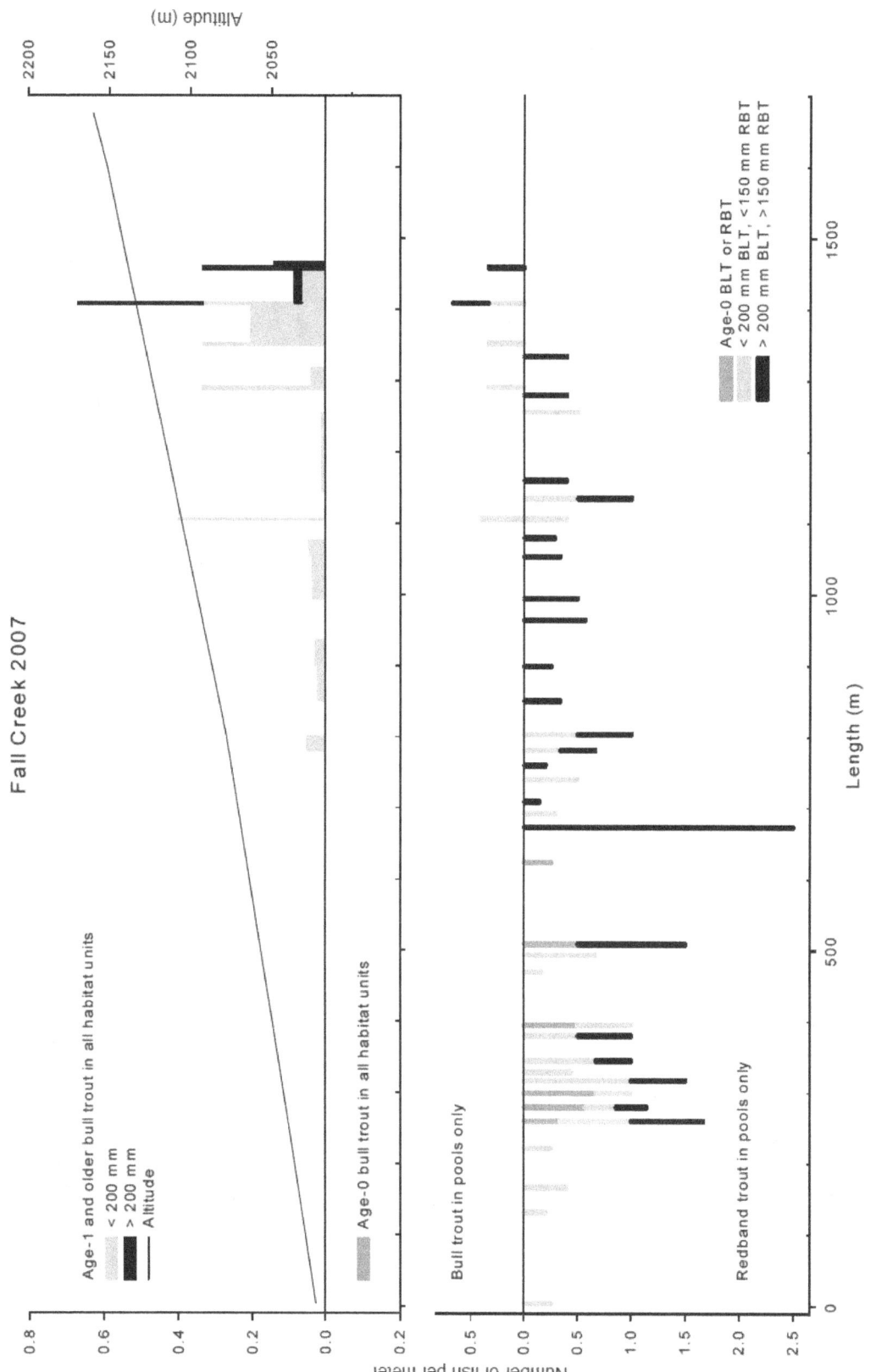

Figure 20. Number of bull trout (BLT) per meter by size class for all habitat units sampled along with altitude (upper graph) and the number of bull trout and redband trout (RBT) per meter by size class in pools only (lower graph) in Fall Creek (rkm 1.4 – 3.2), Nevada, 2007.

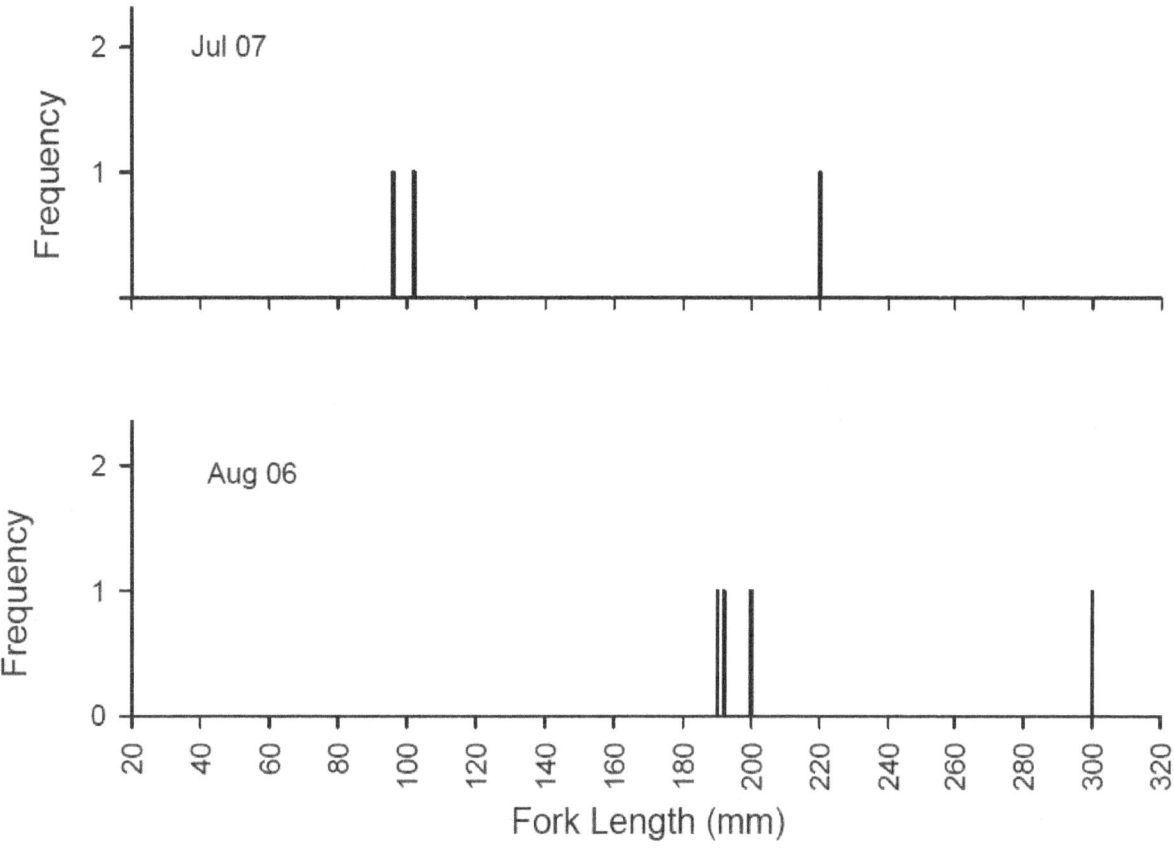

Figure 21. Length frequency in 2-mm increments of all bull trout sampled in Slide Creek of the East Fork Jarbidge River, Nevada, in 2006 and 2007. Sampling effort is not the same for each year.

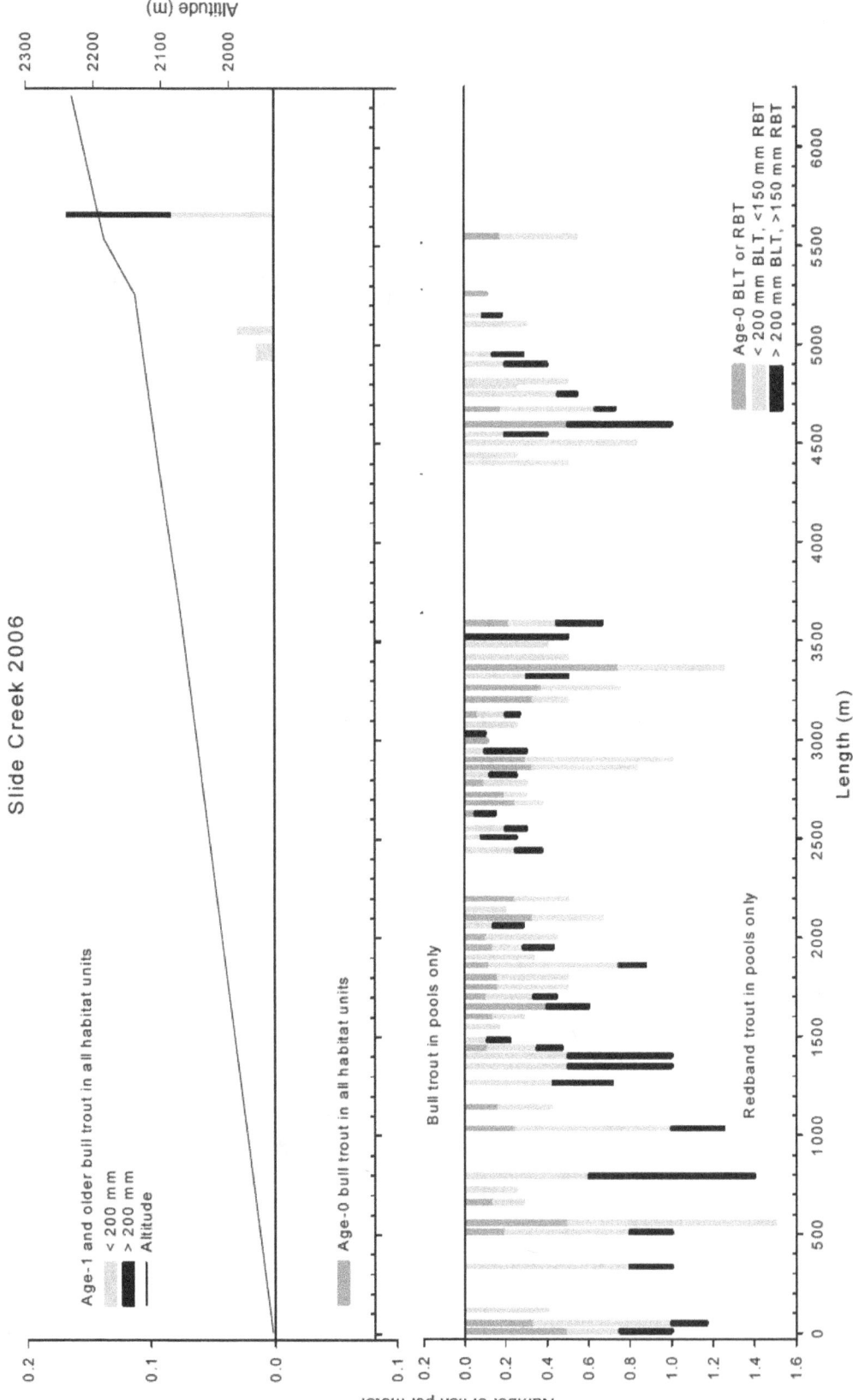

Figure 22. Number of bull trout (BLT) per meter by size class for all habitat units sampled along with altitude (upper graph) and the number of bull trout and redband trout (RBT) per meter by size class in pools only (lower graph) in Slide Creek (rkm 0 – 5.5), Nevada, 2006. NS = not sampled.

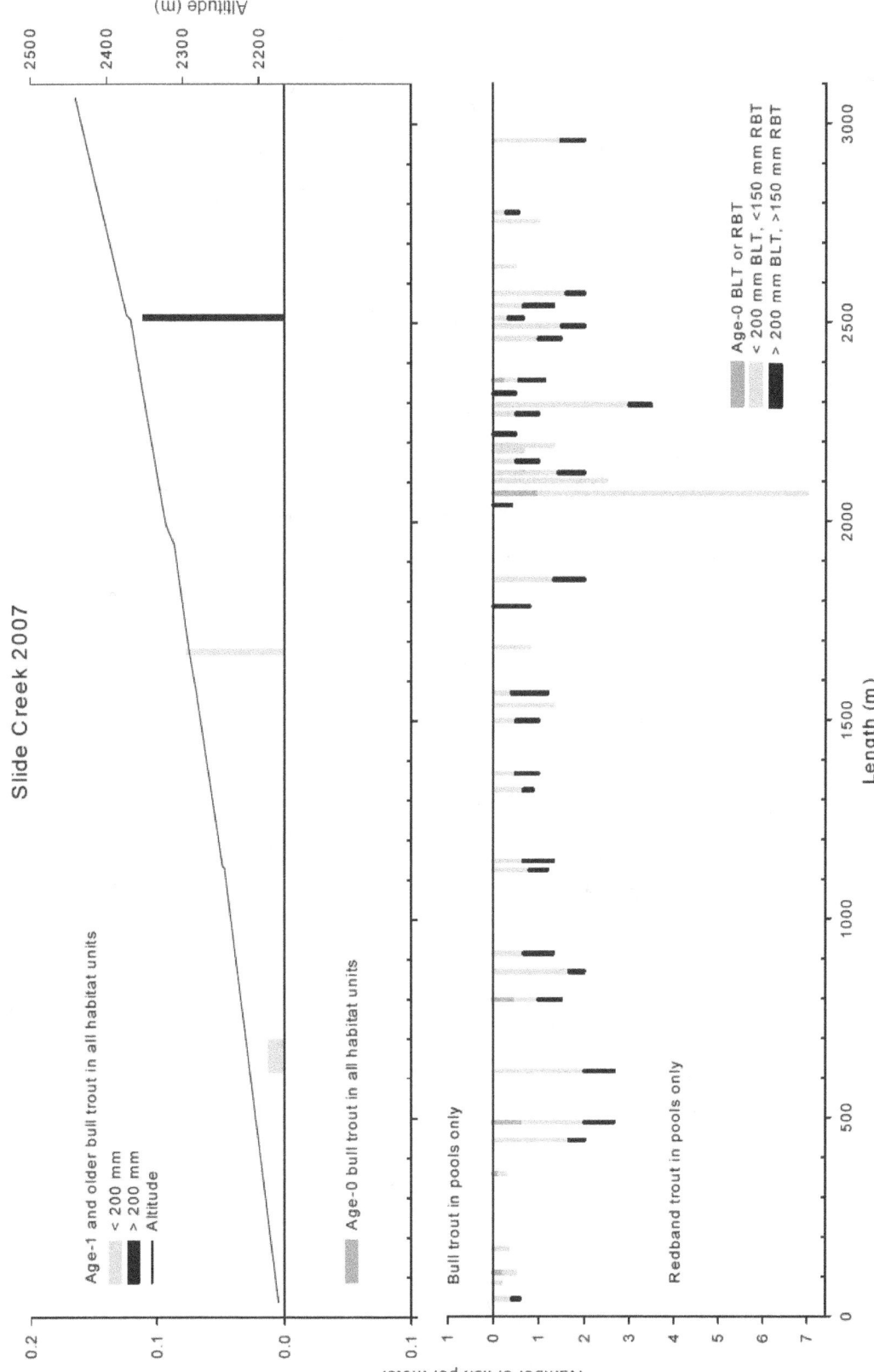

Figure 23. Number of bull trout (BLT) per meter by size class for all habitat units sampled along with altitude (upper graph) and the number of bull trout and redband trout (RBT) per meter by size class in pools only (lower graph) in Slide Creek (rkm 4.6 – 7.7), Nevada, 2007. NS = not sampled.

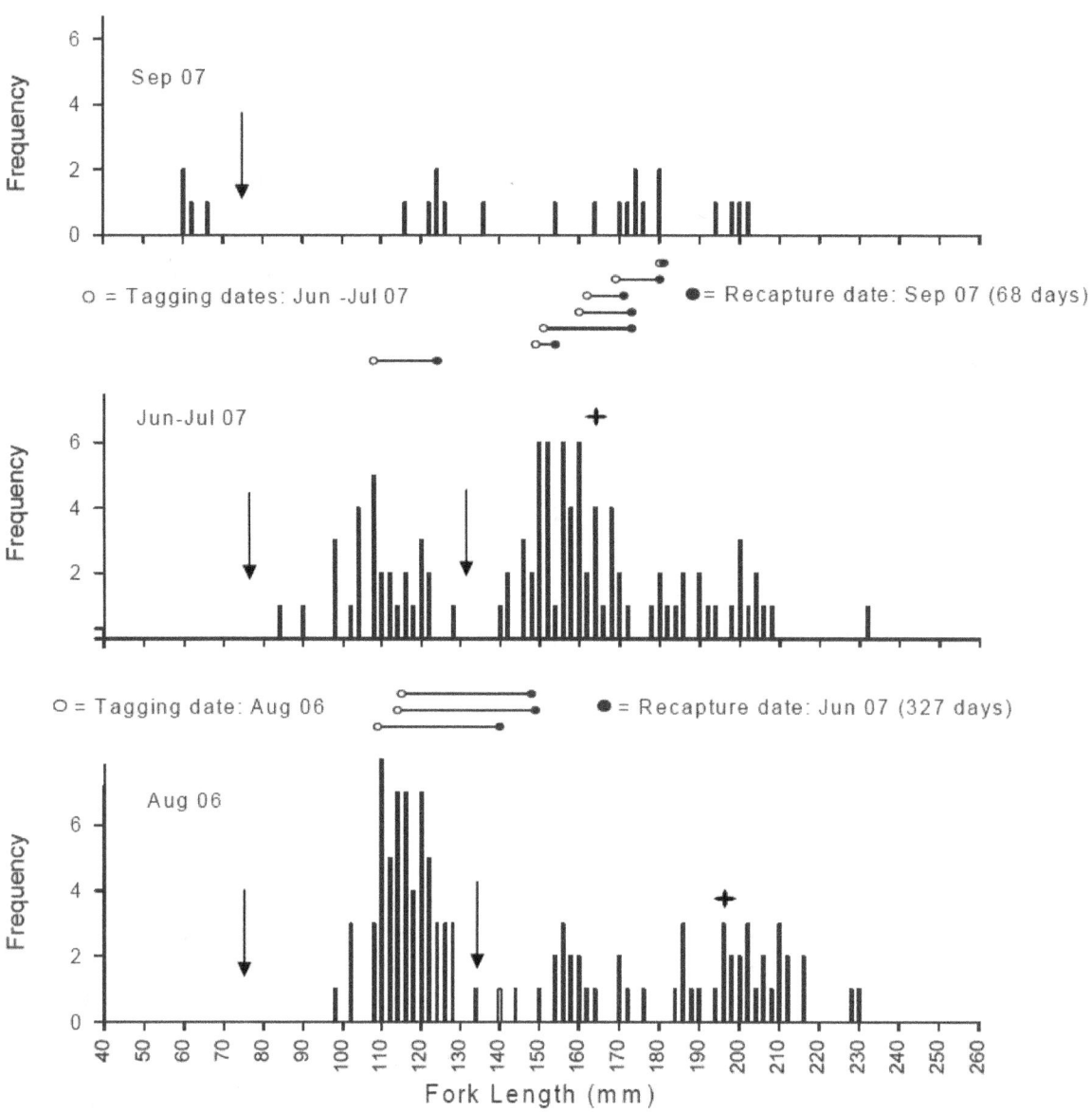

Figure 24. Length frequency in 2-mm increments of all bull trout sampled in Dave Creek of the East Fork Jarbidge River, Nevada, in summer 2006, early summer 2007, and late summer 2007. The horizontal lines indicate the growth of individual fish that were tagged in 2006 and recaptured in early summer 2007, and those that were tagged early summer 2007 and recaptured late summer 2007. The number of days between tagging and recapture are shown in parentheses. The symbol "+" indicates the fork length of fish at tagging that were detected at an interrogation site after tagging. Vertical arrows indicate the break between age-0, age-1, and age-2 or older bull trout.

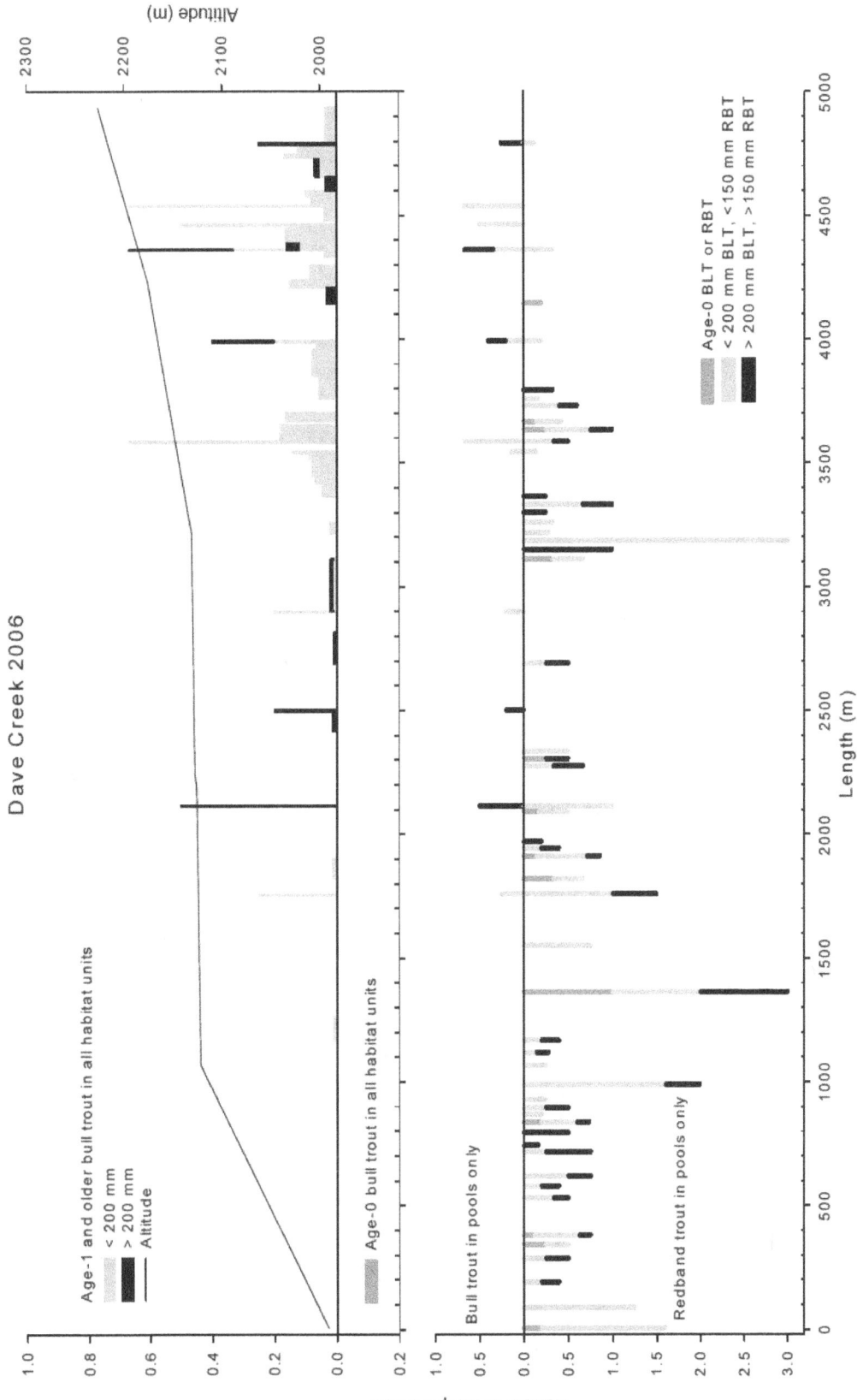

Figure 25. Number of bull trout (BLT) per meter by size class for all habitat units sampled along with altitude (upper graph) and the number of bull trout and redband trout (RBT) per meter by size class in pools only (lower graph) in Dave Creek (rkm 6.8 – 11.7), Nevada, 2006.

49

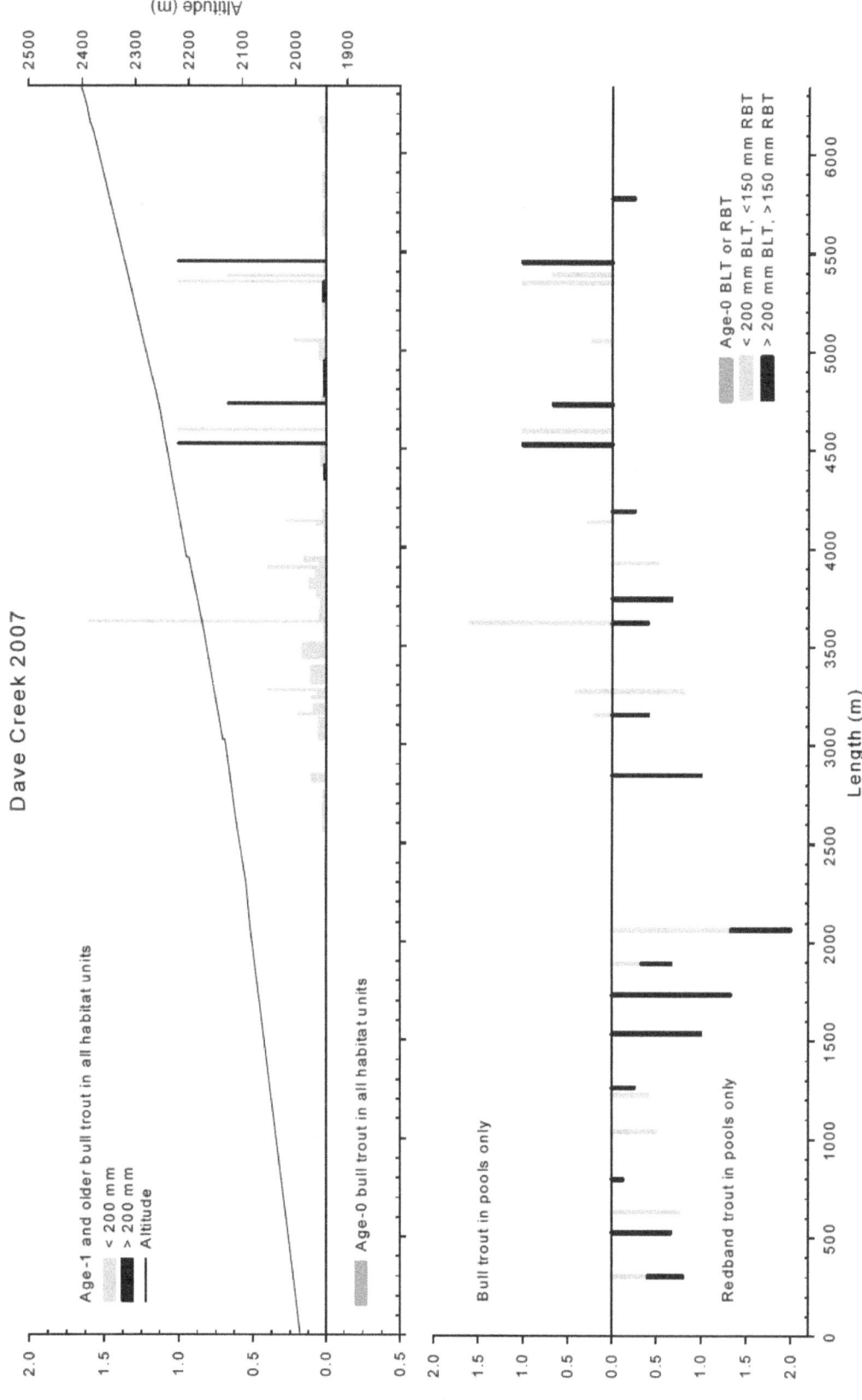

Figure 26. Number of bull trout (BLT) per meter by size class for all habitat units sampled along with altitude (upper graph) and the number of bull trout and redband trout (RBT) per meter by size class in pools only (lower graph) in Dave Creek (rkm 6.8 – 14.0), Nevada, 2007.

50

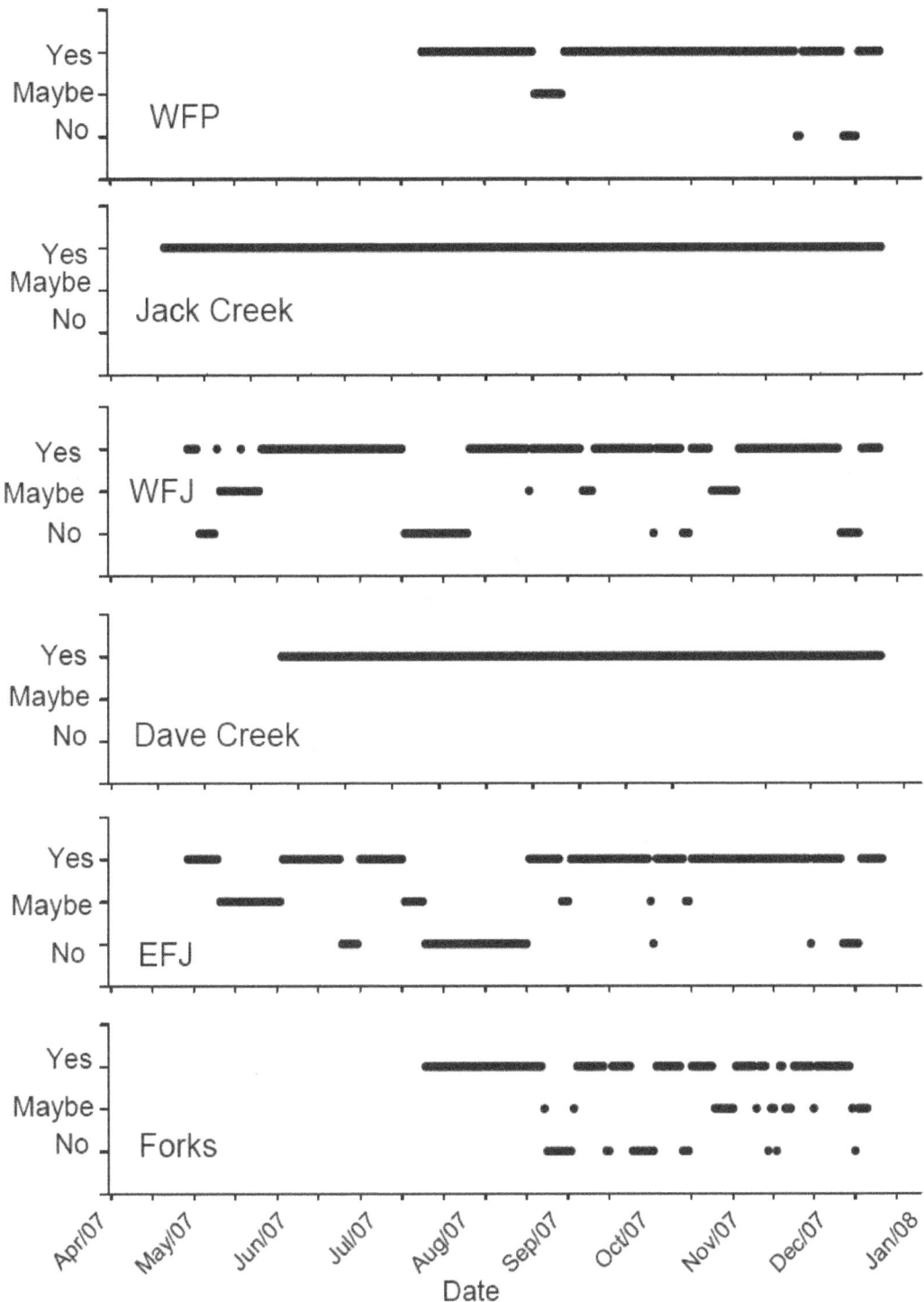

Figure 27. Operational status of interrogation systems during 2007 in the Jarbidge River subbasin, Idaho and Nevada. Maybe indicates that although the system was operational, the distance at which a tag could be detected may have been reduced due to low battery voltage.

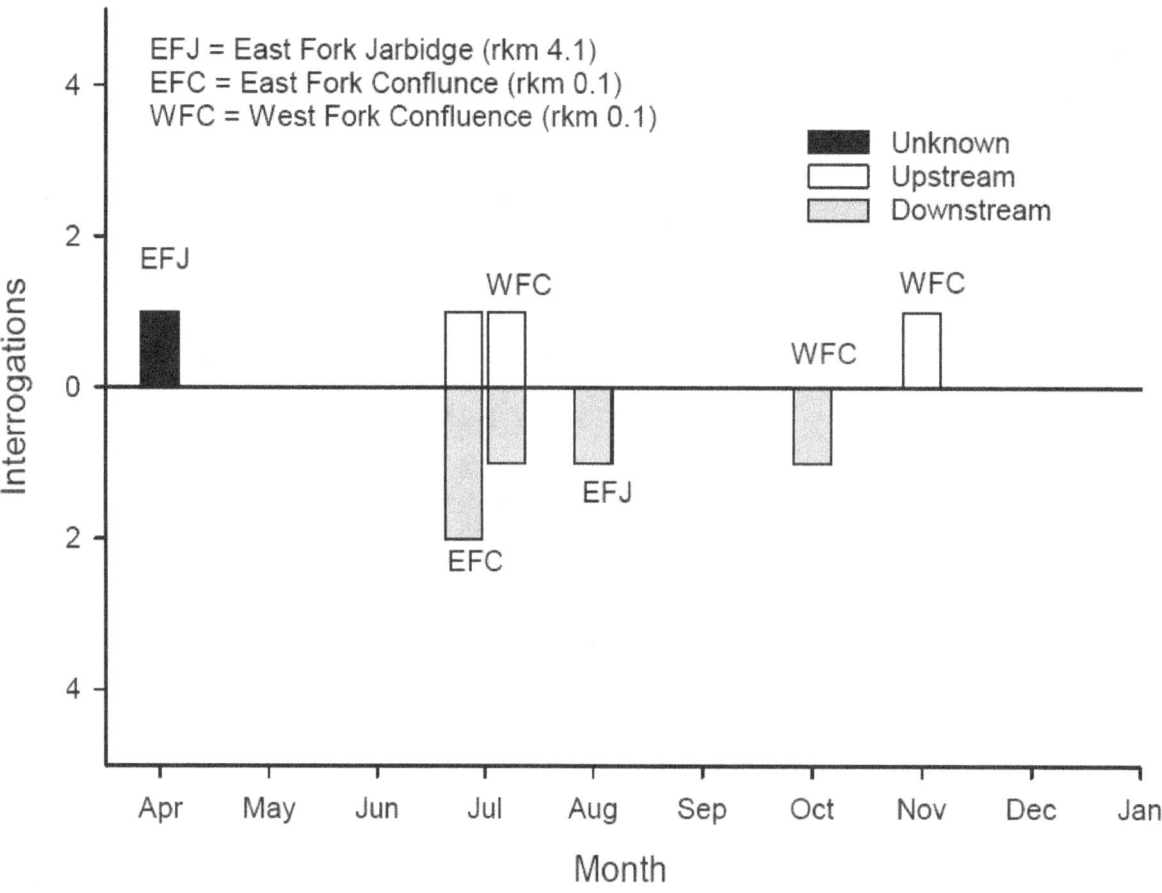

Figure 28. Number and movement direction of PIT tagged bull trout by month detected at the interrogation site in the East Fork Jarbidge River (EFJ, rkm 4.1), Idaho, and at the East Fork Jarbidge River and West Fork Jarbidge River (Forks, rkm 0.1) interrogation sites, Idaho, during 2007.

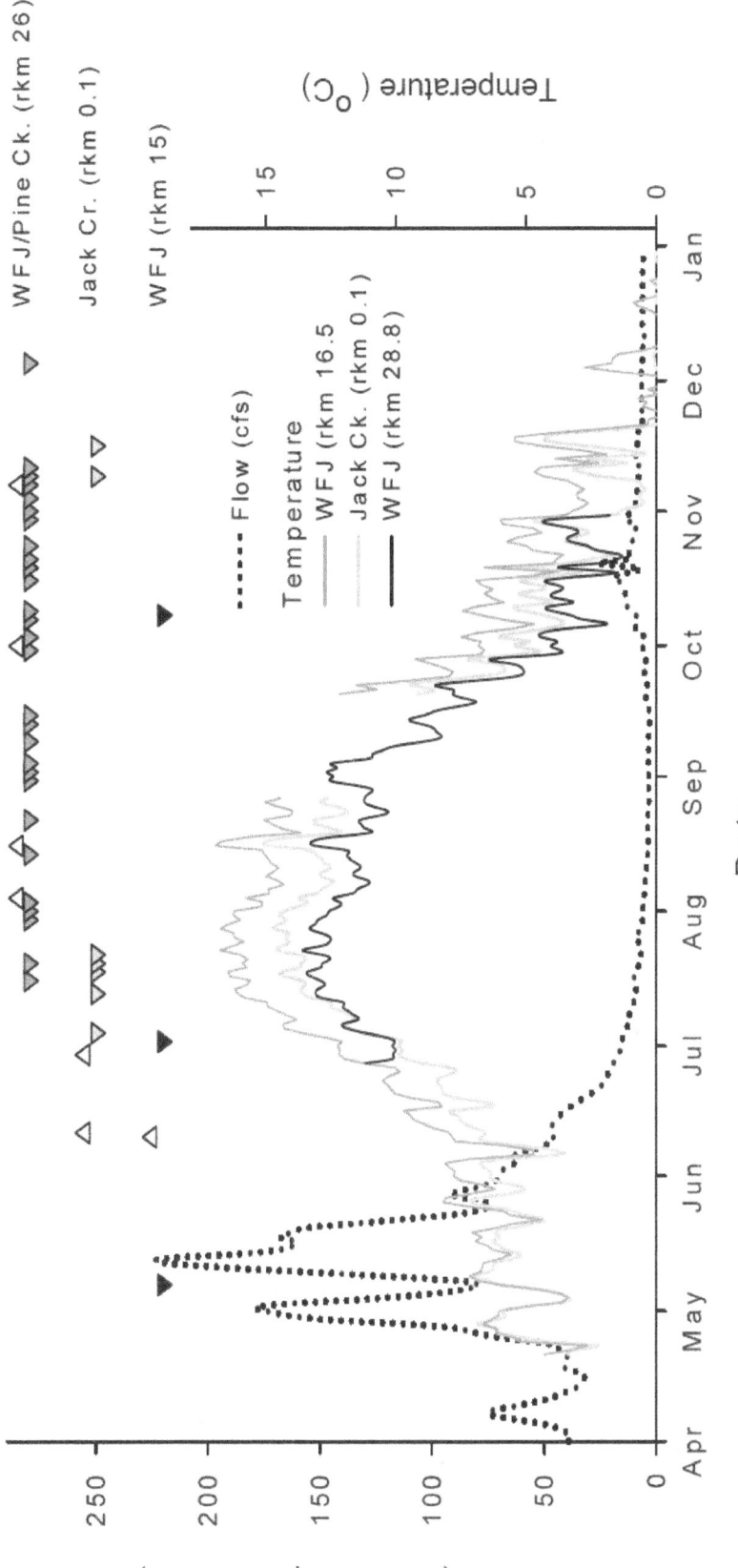

Figure 29. Streamflow (cfs), temperature, and direction of PIT tagged bull trout movements detected at interrogation sites in West Fork Jarbidge River (rkm 15), Jack Creek (rkm 0.1), and West Fork Jarbidge and Pine Creek confluence (rkm 26), Nevada, 2007. Triangles pointing up indicate upstream movement, and triangles pointing down indicate downstream movement. Stream flow measurements were taken from the USGS flow gage on the West Fork Jarbidge River (WFJ, rkm 19.2). Temperatures were taken at rkm 0.1 in Jack Cr., rkm 16.5 of the West Fork Jarbidge River below Jack Cr., and rkm 28.8 in the West Fork Jarbidge River at Snowslide Gulch by BLM.

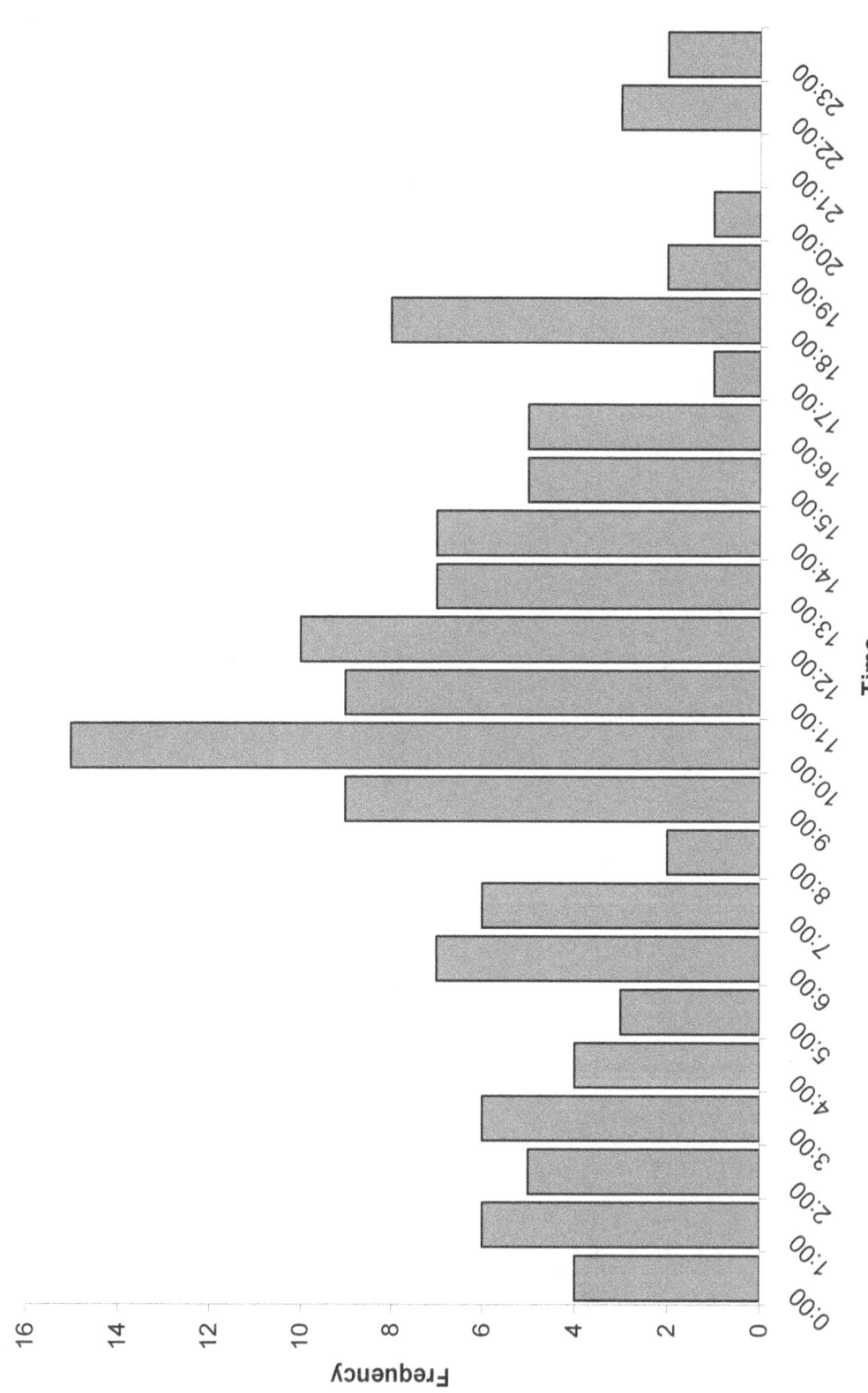

Figure 30. Time of day that PIT tagged bull trout passed any interrogation system in the Jarbidge River subbasin, Idaho and Nevada, in 2006 and 2007.

54

Table 1. Number of bull trout the captured by electrofishing and PIT tagged in the East and West Forks of the Jarbidge River watershed in 2006.

[See figure 3 for additional information on sampling locations. Start and end river kilometer (rkm) were estimated with GPS positions and mapping software. All fish tagged in 2006 were tagged with 12-mm 134.4Khz PIT tags. Bolded numbers represent combined totals by stream for each sampling effort]

Watershed Stream or section	Sampling dates	Rkm (start)	Rkm (end)	Bull trout captured	PIT tags deployed	Genetic samples collected
West Fork Jarbidge River (WFJ)						
Gorge Gulch to just below Sawmill Cr. (WFJ)	7/19-7/22	27.0	30.2	76	73	41
Pine Cr. Campground to Gorge Gulch (WFJ)	8/07, 10/04	23.5	27.0	7	7	5
Bourne Gulch to Pine Cr. campground (WFJ)	9/24-9/26	22.0	23.5	13	13	13
Instream interrogation site (WFJ)	9/23-9/24	14.5	15.5	1	1	1
Mainstem WFJ subtotal				**97**	**94**	**60**
Pine Creek	7/23-9/26	0	6.5	27	25	25
Jack Creek	9/08-9/11	0	4.3	70	66	59
WFJ total		**20.0**		**194**	**185**	**144**
East Fork Jarbidge River (EFJ)						
Dave Creek	8/03-8/06	6.8	11.7	129	111	67
Mainstem wilderness (EFJ)	8/17-8/19	15.6	24.7	13	13	13
Above Murphy Hot Springs (EFJ)	10/03	4.1	4.9	0	0	0
Fall Creek	8/20	0	2.0	9	9	9
Slide Creek				4	4	4
Confluence with EFJ	8/21	0	2.9	0	0	0
Middle	8/22	3.1	4.6	2	2	2
Upper	8/22	5.4	5.5	2	2	2
EFJ total		**19.9**		**155**	**137**	**93**
WFJ and EFJ combined total		**39.9**		**349**	**322**	**237**

Table 2. Number of bull trout captured by electrofishing and PIT tagged in the West Fork Jarbidge River subbasin in 2007.

[See figure 2 for additional information on sampling locations. Start and end river kilometer (rkm) were estimated with GPS positions and mapping software. All fish tagged in 2007 were tagged with 12-mm 134.4Khz PIT tags. Bolded numbers represent combined totals of each sampling effort]

Watershed Stream or section	Sampling dates	Rkm (start)	Rkm (end)	Bull trout captured	PIT tags deployed	Recaptured bull trout from 2006	Genetic samples collected
West Fork Jarbidge River (WFJ)							
WFJ	6/13-6/14 6/20-6/22 6/26, 8/02 8/14-8/15	21.7	32.2	**272**[c]	**258**	**6**	**24**
Pine Creek	8/16, 8/21- 8/23, 8/27, 8/29	0	5.9	**430**	**380**	**5**	**97**
Jack Creek							
Marking sampling effort	8/06-8/07, 8/09	0	5.4	93	70	9	78
Recapture sampling effort	8/08, 8/10	0	5.4	53[a]	31	1[b]	28
Jack Creek subtotal				**146**	**101**	**10**[b]	**106**
Deer Creek	9/10	6.9	9.4	0	0	0	0
Buck Creek	9/14						
Below private property		3.6	3.8	0	0	0	0
Above private property		12.7	13.1	0	0	0	0
Buck Creek subtotal				**0**	**0**	**0**	**0**
WFJ total		24.9[c]		848	739	21	227

[a] Twenty-three bull trout were recaptured from the marking sampling effort the previous day and were not included.
[b] The number of recaptured bull trout does not include fish that were tagged and recaptured within 2007.
[c] Distance does not include areas that were re-sampled.

Table 3. Number of bull trout captured by electrofishing and PIT tagged in the East Fork Jarbidge River subbasin in 2007.

[See figure 3 for additional information on sampling locations. Start and end rkm were estimated with GPS positions and mapping software. All fish tagged in 2007 were tagged with 12-mm 134.4Khz PIT tags. The number of recaptured bull trout does not include fish that were tagged and recaptured within 2007. Bolded numbers represent combined totals by stream for each sampling effort]

Watershed Stream or section	Sampling dates	Rkm (start)	Rkm (end)	Bull trout captured	PIT tags deployed	Recaptured bull trout from 2006	Genetic samples collected
East Fork Jarbidge River (EFJ)							
EFJ							
Below Slide Cr. to Slide Cr.	7/17	23.0	23.5	1	0	1	1
Wilderness (rkm 32.5)	7/12-7/14	32.5	35.0	323	312	0[a]	203
Unnamed East Fork tributary	7/13	0	0.3	13	12	0	8
EFJ subtotal				**337**	**324**	**1**	**212**
Cougar Creek							
Confluence with EFJ	7/11	0	0.7	0	0	0	0
Site 2	7/11	1.2	1.5	1	1	0	1
Site 3 to barrier	7/11-7/12	1.8	3.1	6	6	0	6
Cougar Creek subtotal				**7**	**7**	**0**	**7**
Fall Creek	7/15	1.4	3.2	30	30	0	30
Slide Creek							
Site 1	7/16	4.6	5.7	1	1	0	1
Site 2 to barrier	7/16-7/17	5.8	7.7	2	2	0	2
Slide Creek subtotal				**3**	**3**	**0**	**3**
Gods Pocket Creek	7/17	0.6	0.9	0	0	0	0
Dave Creek							
Initial sampling effort	6/28-7/02	6.8	14.0	105	100	3	81
Recapture sampling effort	9/11	10.5	13.9	23	11	0[b]	8
Dave Creek subtotal				**128**	**111**	**3**	**89**
EFJ total		17.8 [c]		**505**	**475**	**4**	**342**
EFJ and WFJ combined total		42.7 [c]		**1,353**	**1,214**	**25**	**569**

[a] Nine bull trout were recaptured from previous day of 2007 sampling in Wilderness and were not included.

[b] Seven bull trout were recaptured from initial 2007 sampling of Dave Creek and were not included.

[c] Distance does not include areas that were re-sampled.

Table 4. Location, altitude and estimated length of fish and habitat surveys conducted in the Jarbidge River watershed during 2006.

[See figures 2 and 3 for additional information on sampling locations. Altitudes were obtained using Google® Earth as altitudes given by GPS unit were not accurate. Estimated length was calculated by summing the visually estimated lengths of each habitat unit]

Watershed / Stream or section	GPS reading Start of reach		GPS reading End of reach		Altitude (m)		Estimated length (m) [d]
	North	West	North	West	SOR	EOR	
West Fork Jarbidge River							
All sites combined	41°55'49.8"	115°25'04.3"	41°48'07.8"	115°24'12.1"	1,753	2,225	12,854
Gorge Gulch - below Sawmill Creek	41°49'56.5"	115°25'17.9"	41°48'07.8"	115°24'12.1"	2,062	2,225	4,389
Pine Creek camp - Gorge Gulch	41°50'03.1"	115°25'30.6"	41°50'03.7"	115°25'38.6"	2,039	2,062	1,431
Bourne Gulch - Pine Creek camp	41°52'09.2"	115°25'58.6"	41°50'03.1"	115°25'30.6"	1,890	2,039	4,822
Antenna site	41°55'49.8"	115°25'04.3"	41°54'54.1"	115°25'27.8"	1,753	1,826	2,213
Pine Creek	41°50'03.1"	115°25'30.6"	41°47'05.4"	115°27'27.4"	2,039	2,388	5,529
Jack Creek	41°54'39.2"	115°25'22.6"	41°53'23.7"	115°23'07.7"	1,673	2,138	5,224
East Fork Jarbidge River							
All sites combined	RNT[a]	RNT	41°47'30.0"	115°19'21.8"	RNT	2,235	8,821
Above Murphy	RNT		RNT		RNT	RNT	820
Wilderness	41°51'59.6"	115°18'45.8"	41°47'30.0"	115°19'21.8"	1,962	2,235	8,003
Slide Creek	41°52'00.0"	115°18'45.9"	41°50'16.1"	115°15'59.8"	1,958	2,252	4,601
Fall Creek	41°51'22.6"	115°18'52.8"	RNT		1,944	2,073	2,310
Dave Creek	41°56'27.0"	115°22'08.9"	41°54'00.3"	115°20'58.7"	1,986	2,261	4,900
Total length surveyed							**44,437**

[a] RNT=GPS reading not taken because of topography of basin. Values were estimated from Google® Earth.

Table 5. Location, altitude and estimated length of fish and habitat surveys conducted in the Jarbidge River watershed during 2007.

[See figures 2 and 3 for additional information on sampling locations. Altitudes were obtained using Google® Earth as altitudes given by GPS unit were not accurate. Estimated length was calculated by summing the visually estimated lengths of each habitat unit]

Watershed Stream or section	GPS reading Start of reach		GPS reading End of reach		Altitude (m)		Estimated length (m)
	North	West	North	West	SOR	EOR	
West Fork Jarbidge River (WFJ)							
WFJ	41°52'09.9"	115°25'55.2"	41°47'34.4"	115°23'47.3"	1,900	2,317	8,871
Pine Creek	41°50'03.4"	115°25'31.1"	41°47'24.8"	115°27'00.5"	2,009	2,326	4,490
Jack Creek	41°54'43.1"	115°25'29.0"	41°52'53.1"	115°22'47.5"	1,795	2,270	5,347
Deer Creek	41°52'43.8"	115°27'07.5"	41°51'42.0"	115°28'01.6"	2,143	2,267	1,754
Buck Creek							
Below private property	41°58'28.2"	115°25'44.1"	41°58'52.2"	115°25'57.6"	1,834	1,836	163
Above private property	41°54'40.5"	115°28'52.1"	41°54'32.0"	115°29'01.3"	2,046	2,058	352
East Fork Jarbidge River (EFJ)							
EFJ below Slide Creek to Slide Creek confluence	41°52'10.7"	115°18'48.4"	41°51'59.2"	115°18'45.5"	1,930	1,938	588
Upper EFJ	41°47'26.5"	115°19'21.6"	41°46'59.9"	115°20'45.1"	2,244	2,419	2,709
Cougar Creek							
Confluence with EFJ	41°50'24.3"	115°19'12.8"	41°50'19.8"	115°19'38.9"	2,004	2,044	665
Site 2	41°50'04.4"	115°19'47.9"	41°49'52.5"	115°19'52.7"	2,076	2,100	511
Site 3 to barrier	41°49'44.9"	115°19'55.8"	41°49'04.3"	115°20'10.1"	2,126	2,284	1,453
Dave Creek	41°56'26.9"	115°22'09.1"	41°52'56.0"	115°21'18.9"	1,991	2,402	6,340
Fall Creek	41°50'55.5"	115°19'38.2"	41°50'11.8"	115°20'19.1"	2,022	2,181	1,675
Slide Creek							
Site 1	41°50'22.2"	115°16'37.9"	41°50'18.1"	115°15'58.6"	2,175	2,248	1,133
Site 2 to barrier	41°50'18.9"	115°15'52.6"	41°51'04.8"	115°15'12.5"	2,249	2,442	1,933
Gods Pocket Creek	41°50'37.1"	115°17'46.1"	41°50'26.6"	115°17'51.0"	2,120	2,146	498
Unnamed East Fork Tributary	41°46'56.7"	115°19'46.4"	41°46'46.4"	115°19'47.9"	2,318	2,360	248

Table 6. Number (*n*) of bull trout captured, the sampling distance (rkm), the number of bull trout captured with a fork length greater than 200 mm, the number of bull trout with a fork length greater than 250 mm, the minimum (min) fork length, the maximum (max) fork length, and weight of bull trout for each creek sampled in the Jarbidge River watershed, Nevada, in 2006-2007.

[The number of fish captured does not include fish that were tagged and recaptured within 2007. Figures 2 and 3 contain additional location information. River kilometer (rkm) was estimated, using mapping software, from a start point of the confluence of the East Fork and West Fork Jarbidge River, or for tributaries, the confluence with East Fork or West Fork Jarbidge River]

Watershed	River kilometer (rkm)			No. with fork length		Fork length (mm)		Weight (g)	
Stream	(start)	(end)	*n*	>200mm	>250mm	min	max	min	max
West Fork Jarbidge River (WFJ)-2006									
WFJ [a]	14.5	30.2	97	11	3	23	330	0.3	508.0
Pine Cr.	0	6.6	27	6	0	39	243	0.7	161.0
Jack Cr.	0	4.3	70	8	3	61	310	2.5	268.0
		Total	**194**	**25**	**6**				
West Fork Jarbidge River (WFJ)-2007									
WFJ	24.8	32.2	272	19	3	28	273	3.6	222.8
Pine Cr.	0	5.9	430	12	3	55	387	1.8	650.3
Jack Cr.	0	5.4	146	14	2	42	283	1.0	230.8
		Total	**848**	**45**	**8**				
East Fork Jarbidge River (EFJ)-2006									
EFJ	16.0	22.6	13	5	1	135	260	22.4	194.5
Dave Cr.	6.8	11.7	129	16	0	97	229	9.3	148.0
Fall Cr.	0	2.0	9	0	1	119	360 [b]	16.1	440.6
Slide Cr. [a]	0	2.1	4	0	1	189	300	62.8	230.2
		Total	**155**	**21**	**3**				
East Fork Jarbidge River (EFJ)-2007									
EFJ [a]	23.0	35.0	324	63	8	78	400 [b]	4.7	767.2
Dave Cr.	6.8	14.0	128	7	0	59	232	1.8	145.4
Fall Cr.	1.4	3.2	30	4	0	79	247	4.8	196.9
Slide Cr. [a]	4.6	7.7	3	1	0	95	220	8.7	122.7
Cougar Cr. [a]	0	3.1	7	4	2	138	340	26.5	420.4
EFJ Trib.	0	0.3	13	6	0	130	238	20.7	176.9
		Total	**505**	**85**	**10**				

[a] River kilometer represents the overall range of where sampling occurred. The entire distance was not completely sampled, as certain sections of river were skipped; see figures 2 and 3 for details.

[b] Largest fish captured in Fall Ck. in 2006 and the largest fish captured in the East Fork Jarbidge River in 2007 was the same fish.

Table 7. Number (*n*) of bull trout (BLT) collected, survey length, percent of stream length with bull trout, the percent of habitat units with at least one bull trout, the percent of stream length that was pool-like, and percent of bull trout found in pools in the Jarbidge River watershed in 2006-2007.

[River kilometer was estimated, using mapping software, from a start point of the confluence of the East Fork and West Fork Jarbidge River, or for tributaries, the confluence with either the East Fork or West Fork Jarbidge River. Habitat units were defined as either pool or non-pool]

Watershed		River kilometer		Survey length (m)	% length with BLT	% habitat units with BLT	% length identified as pools	% BLT in pools
Stream	*n*	(start)	(end)					
West Fork Jarbidge River (WFJ)-2006								
WFJ [a]	97	14.5	30.2	12,856	20	21	16	20
Pine Cr.	27	0	6.6	5,530	21	14	10	30
Jack Cr.	70	0	4.3	5,224	24	29	10	44
West Fork Jarbidge River (WFJ)-2007								
WFJ	272	24.8	32.2	8,872	37	50	12	15
Pine Cr.	430	0	5.9	4,490	57	83	9	10
Jack Cr.	146	0	5.4	5,347	27	45	8	39
East Fork Jarbidge River (EFJ)-2006								
EFJ	13	16.0	22.6	8,003	8	5	19	25
Dave Cr.	129	6.8	11.7	4,903	38	46	7	15
Fall Cr.	9	0	2.0	2,311	15	8	14	22
Slide Cr. [a]	4	0	2.1	4,625	3	3	12	0
East Fork Jarbidge River (EFJ)-2007								
EFJ [a]	324	23.0	35.0	3,297	52	83	13	19
Dave Cr.	128	6.8	14.0	6,340	41	62	2	10
Fall Cr.	30	1.4	3.2	1,675	26	28	9	20
Slide Cr. [a]	3	4.6	7.7	3,066	3	3	4	0
Cougar Cr. [a]	7	0	3.1	2,612	6	4	16	71
Unnamed Trib.	13	0	0.3	248	63	72	5	0

[a] River kilometer represents the overall range of where sampling occurred. The entire distance was not completely sampled, as certain sections of river were skipped; see figures 2 and 3 for more detail.

Table 8. Location and installation date of passive integrated transponder (PIT) tag interrogation units installed in the Jarbidge River watershed in 2006-2007, and the number of bull trout (BLT) interrogated by tagging location in 2006-2007.

[River kilometer was estimated, using mapping software, from a start point of the confluence of the East Fork and West Fork Jarbidge River, or for tributaries, the confluence with either the East Fork or West Fork Jarbidge River. The 4 out of 8 tagging streams listed were the only ones that had fish detected at the interrogators. Fish detected on more than one array are counted more than once]

| Watershed | | River | No. of BLT detected by tagging stream | | | |
| Interrogation site | Start date | kilometer | WFJ | | | EFJ |
			WFJ	Pine Cr.	Jack Cr.	Dave Cr.
West Fork Jarbidge River (WFJ) - 2006						
Jack Creek	9/15/2006	0.1	0	0	1	0
WFJ downstream of Jack Cr.	9/15/2006	15.0	3	1	1	0
West Fork Jarbidge River (WFJ) - 2007						
WFJ at Pine Creek	7/16/2007	26.2	20[a]	8[b]	0	0
Pine Creek at WFJ	7/16/2007	0.1	11	8[b]	0	0
Jack Creek	4/18/2007	0.1	0	0	7	0
WFJ downstream of Jack Cr.	4/28/2007	15.0	1	0	2	0
WFJ at Forks	7/17/2007	0.1	0	0	3[c]	1[c]
East Fork Jarbidge River (EFJ) - 2006						
EFJ at Murphy Hot Springs	9/15/2006	4.1	0	0	0	0
East Fork Jarbidge River (EFJ) - 2007						
Dave Creek	5/23/2007	0.4	0	0	0	0
EFJ at Murphy Hot Springs	4/28/2007	4.1	0	0	1	1
EFJ at Forks	7/17/2007	0.1	0	0	2[c]	1[c]
Total unique fish - 2006			3	1	1	0
Total unique fish - 2007			24	9	9	2

[z] Eighteen of these 20 fish were interrogated moving downstream. The West Fork Jarbidge River/Pine Cr. PTIS detected a fish on the first day of installation.

[d] Seven of these 8 fish were interrogated moving out of Pine Creek and downstream in the West Fork Jarbidge River between 7 Oct. 2007 and 4 Nov. 2007.

[e] One fish from Jack Creek and one from Dave Creek were detected at both the East Fork and West Fork Jarbidge River antennas at the Forks, see figures A2 and A10 for details.

Table 9. Stream discharge in the Jarbidge River watershed on sampling dates in 2007.

[Discharge measurements were taken at passive integrated transponder tag interrogation unit (PTIS) sites]

Subbasin	Discharge, in cubic feet per second		
Stream and location	8/1/07	8/13/07	8/20/07
West Fork Jarbidge River (WFJ)			
Mainstem Jarbidge River below the Forks (rkm 46.6)	30.75	not taken	9.33
WFJ above PTIS (rkm 15.0)	7.86	6.25	4.73
Jack Creek below PTIS (rkm 0.1)	1.39	1.07	0.77
WFJ below Pine Creek (rkm 26.2)	5.42	3.89	3.60
Pine Creek above PTIS (rkm 0.1)	2.44	0.80	1.17
East Fork Jarbidge River (EFJ)			
EFJ above PTIS (rkm 4.1)	18.78	not taken	4.84
Dave Creek above PTIS (rkm 0.4)	0.56	0.38	0.25

Appendix table and figures

Appendix Table A1. Temperatures (ºC) collected with a hand held thermometer while electrofishing in the upper Jarbidge River subbasin, Nevada, during 2006 and 2007.

[Please see tables 1-4 and figures 2 and 3 for specific location information]

Site	Date	Morning (8:00am-11:30am)	Mid (11:30am -2:00pm)	Afternoon (2:00pm-5:00 pm)
Buck Cr.	9/14/2007	9.0		14.0
Cougar Cr.	7/11/2007	12.5		
	7/12/2007	11.5	15.5	
Dave Cr.	8/03/2006		14.0	
	8/04/2006		15.0	
	8/05/2006	8.0	10.0	
	8/06/2006	7.0	10.5	
	6/28/2007	6.0	11.0	13.5
	6/29/2007	5.0	10.5	10.0
	6/30/2007	4.0	9.0	7.0
	7/01/2007	9.0	11.5	
	7/02/2007	7.5	13.0	14.0
	9/06/2007	6.5	9.0	12.0
Deer Cr.	9/10/2007	4.0	7.5	
East Fork Jarbidge River	8/17/2006		11.5	14.0
	8/18/2006	9.5		13.0
	8/19/2006		10.0	9.5
	7/12/2007	9.0		12.0
	7/13/2007	9.0	14.0	15.0
	7/14/2007		15.0	
Fall Cr.	8/20/2006	8.0	9.5	
	7/15/2007			13.0
Gods Pocket Cr.	7/17/2007	10.5		
Jack Cr.	9/08/2006	9.0		
	9/09/2006	9.0	10.0	9.5
	9/11/2006		8.0	
	8/06/2007	13.0	13.5	
	8/07/2007	10.5	10.5	12.0
	8/08/2007	10.0		12.5
	8/09/2007	11.0	13.0	16.0
	8/09/2007	11.0		
	8/10/2007	11.5		14.5
	9/11/2007	6.0	7.0	
Pine Cr.	7/23/2006		13.5	14.5
	7/24/2006	11.0	11.5	
	7/25/2006	10.0	12.5	
	7/26/2006		14.0	
Pine Cr.	8/21/2007	11.0	12.0	

Site	Date	Morning (8:00am-11:30am)	Mid (11:30am -2:00pm)	Afternoon (2:00pm-5:00 pm)
	8/22/2007		11.5	13.5
	8/23/2007	8.0	10.5	12.5
	8/27/2007	10.0		14.5
	8/29/2007	10.0	12.0	14.0
Slide Cr.	8/21/2006			12.0
	8/22/2006	8.0	9.5	
	7/16/2007	12.0	13.0	14.0
West Fork Jarbidge River	7/19/2006		12.0	
	7/20/2006	10.0	12.5	
	7/21/2006	9.5	12.5	
	7/22/2006	10.0	12.0	12.5
	8/07/2006	10.0	11.5	
	9/23/2006		8.0	
	9/24/2006		7.0	
	9/25/2006	5.0	7.0	
	10/04/2006	6.0		
	6/11/2007		10.0	
	6/13/2007	7.5	12.0	
	6/14/2007		9.5	13.0
	6/20/2007	7.0	8.0	
	6/21/2007	6.0	8.5	
	6/22/2007	6.5	8.0	9.0
	6/26/2007	5.0	10.0	12.0
	6/27/2007	6.0	14.0	12.5
	8/02/2007	14.0		16.0
	8/14/2007	11.0	13.0	
	8/15/2007	10.5	11.0	

Appendix Figures A1 – A50. Maps of tagging location and the timing and location of detection or recapture for all bull trout with noteworthy movements during 2006 and 2007 in the Jarbidge River subbasin, Nevada and Idaho.

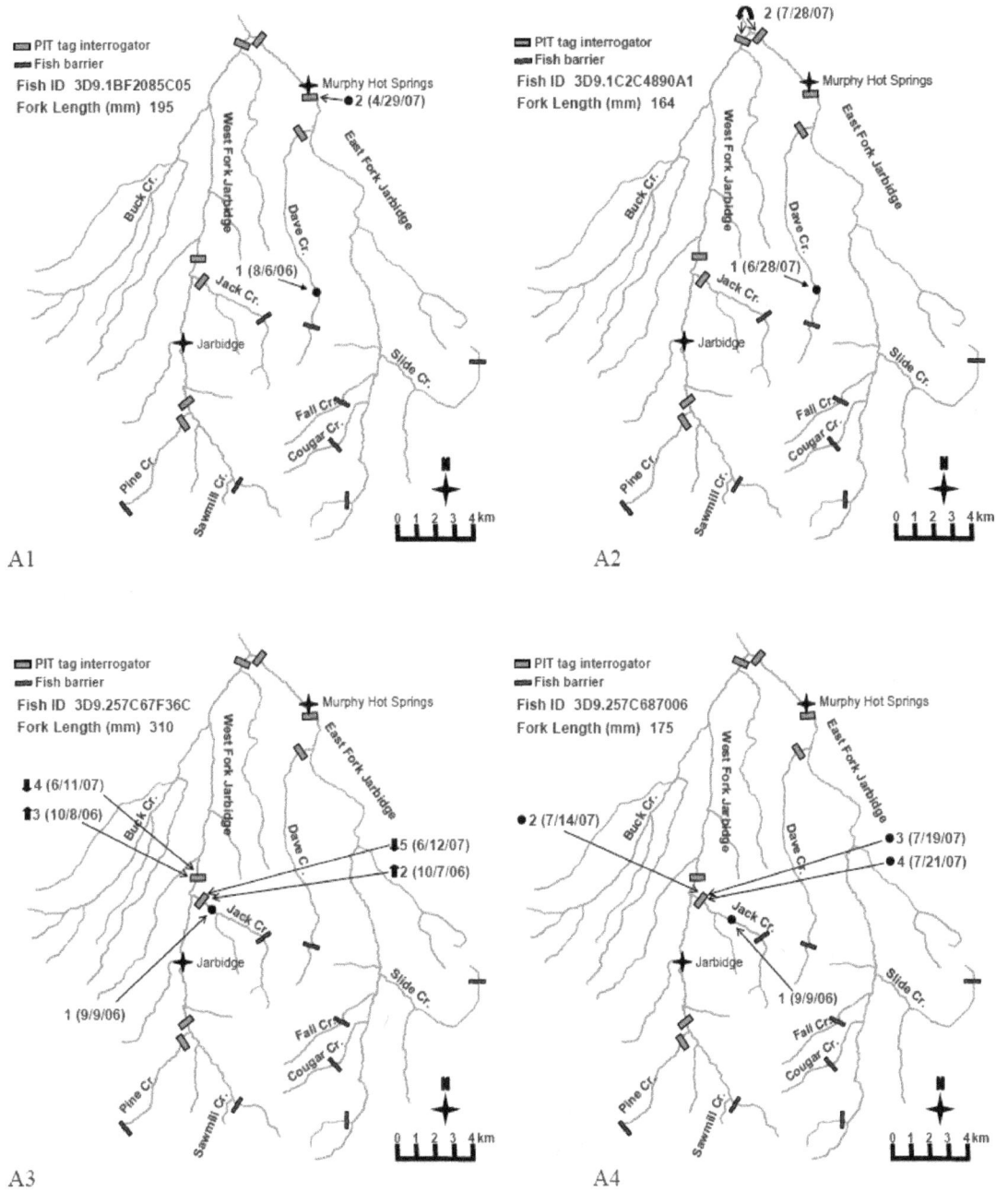

Figures A1 – A4. Movement of PIT-tagged bull trout within the Jarbidge River subbasin in 2006 and 2007. Each map represents a single bull trout and the number next to the symbol represents the order of events (1 = tagging, 2 = interrogation or recapture, 3 + = subsequent interrogation or recapture). See table 8 and figures 28 and 29 for installation dates and summaries of interrogation information.

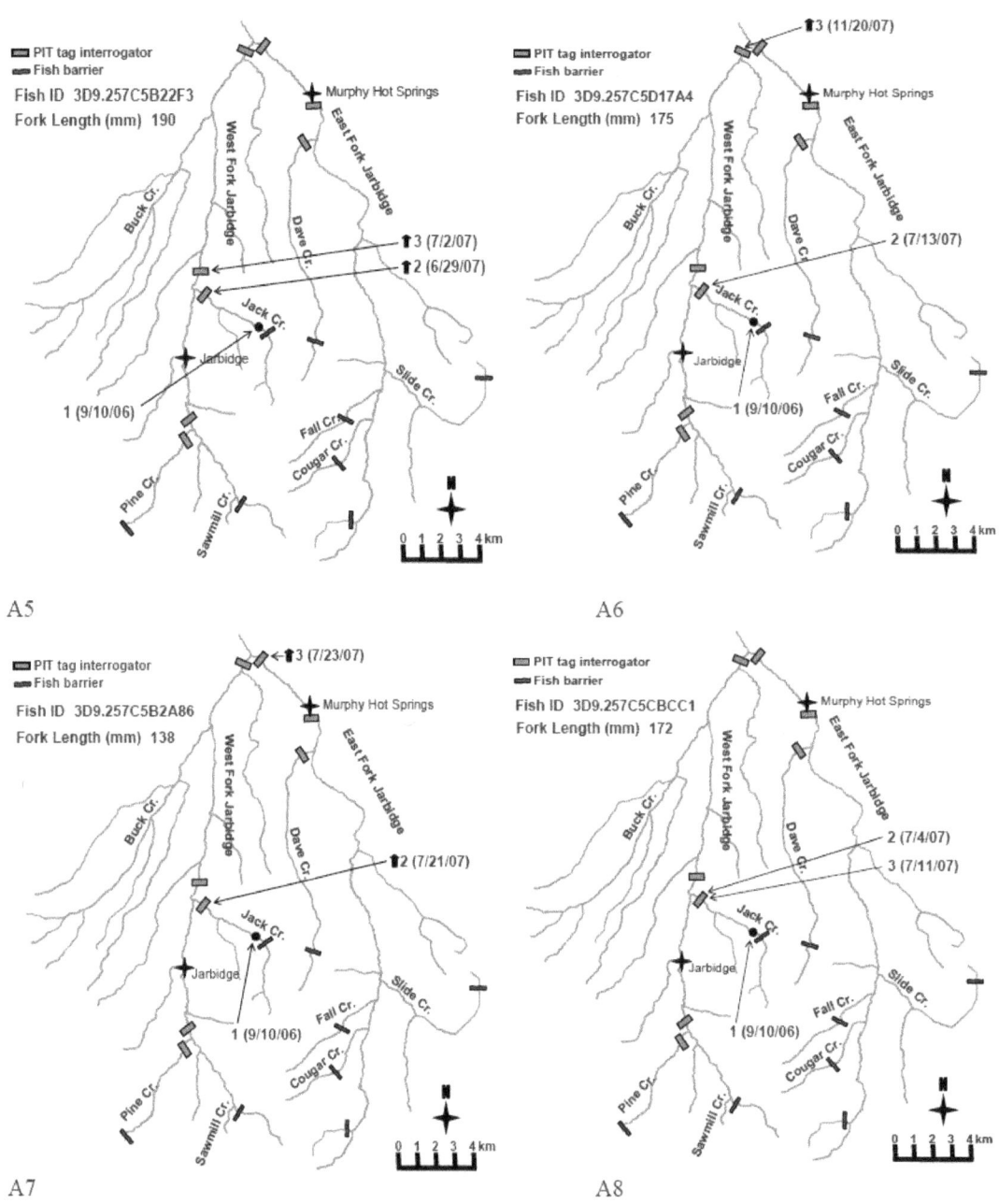

A5

A6

A7

A8

Figures A5 – A8. Movement of PIT-tagged bull trout within the Jarbidge River subbasin in 2006 and 2007. Each map represents a single bull trout and the number next to the symbol represents the order of events (1 = tagging, 2 = interrogation or recapture, 3 + = subsequent interrogation or recapture). See table 8 and figures 28 and 29 for installation dates and summaries of interrogation information.

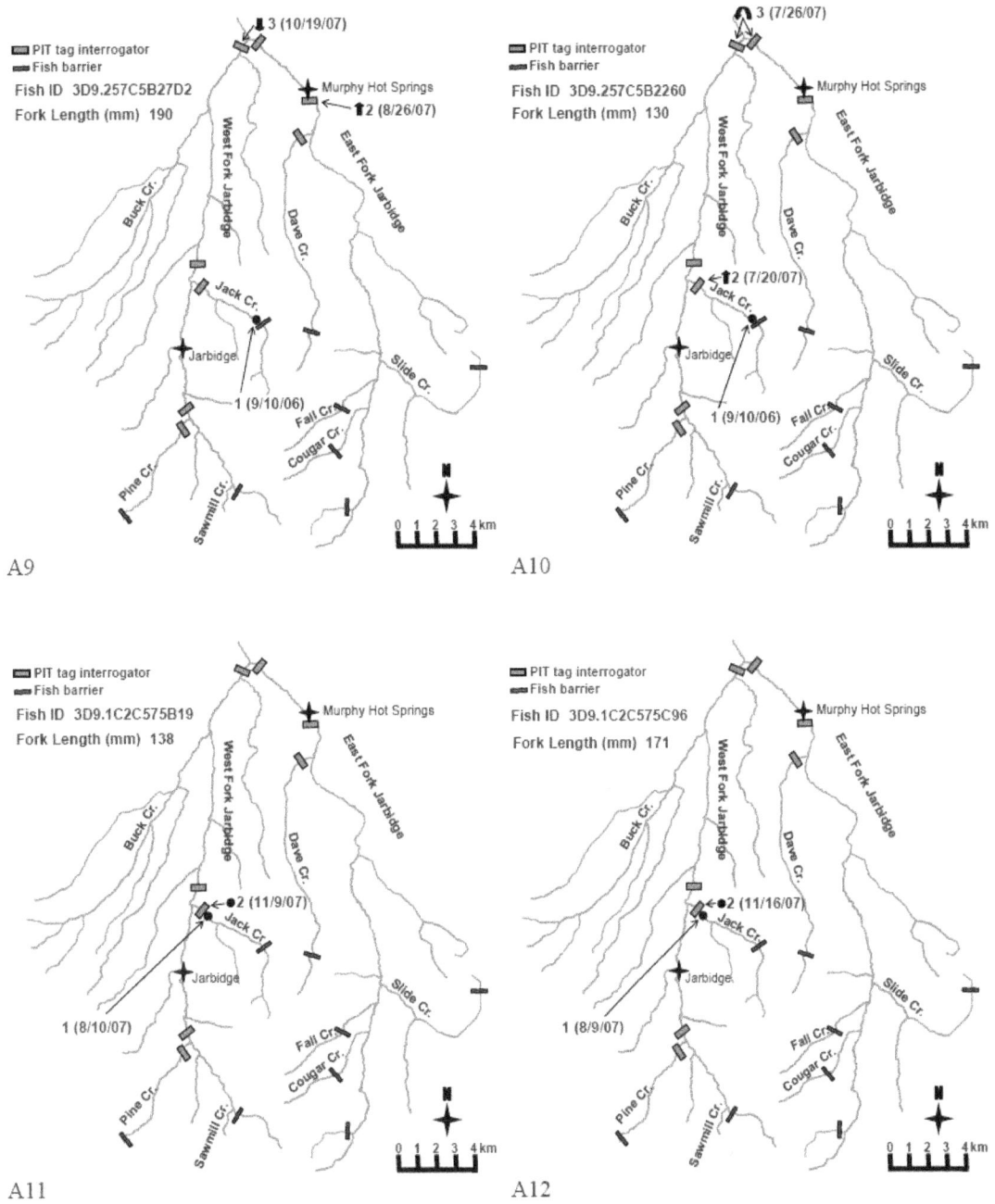

Figures A9 – A12. Movement of PIT-tagged bull trout within the Jarbidge River subbasin in 2006 and 2007. Each map represents a single bull trout and the number next to the symbol represents the order of events (1 = tagging, 2 = interrogation or recapture, 3 + = subsequent interrogation or recapture). See table 8 and figures 28 and 29 for installation dates and summaries of interrogation information.

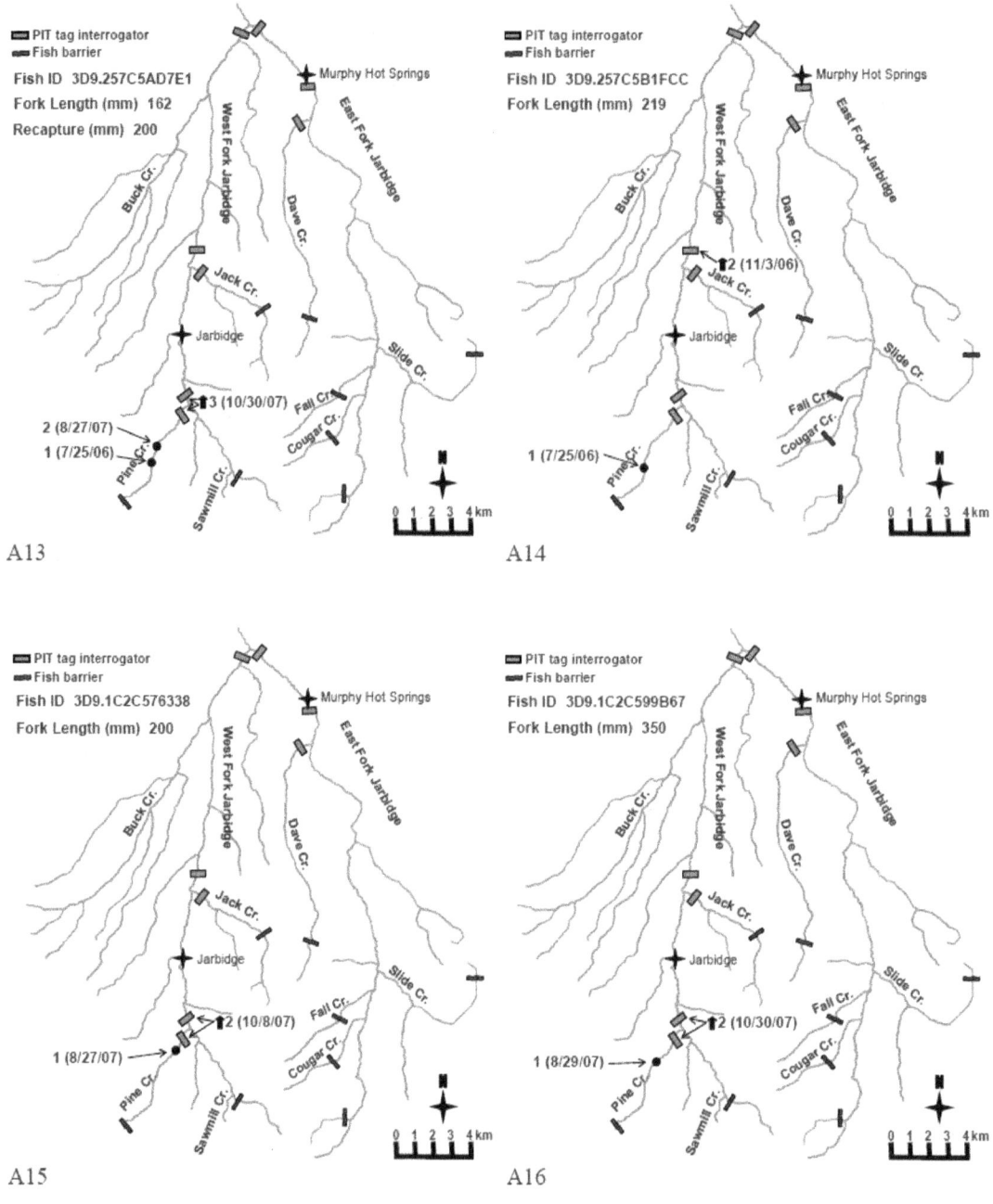

Figures A13 – A16. Movement of PIT-tagged bull trout within the Jarbidge River subbasin in 2006 and 2007. Each map represents a single bull trout and the number next to the symbol represents the order of events (1 = tagging, 2 = interrogation or recapture, 3 + = subsequent interrogation or recapture). See table 8 and figures 28 and 29 for installation dates and summaries of interrogation information.

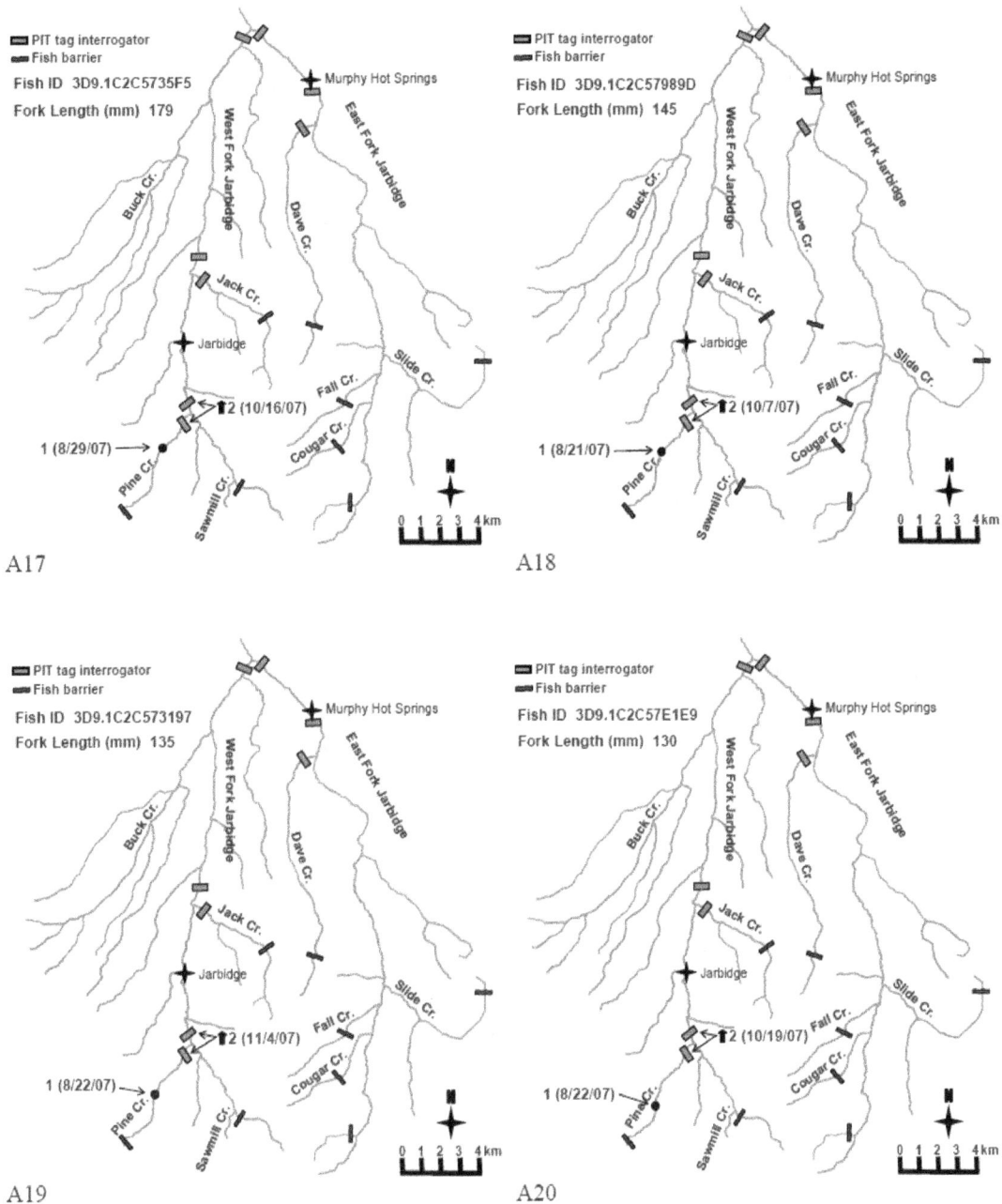

Figures A17 – A20. Movement of PIT-tagged bull within the Jarbidge River subbasin in 2006 and 2007. Each map represents a single bull trout and the number next to the symbol represents the order of events (1 = tagging, 2 = interrogation or recapture, 3 + = subsequent interrogation or recapture). See table 8 and figures 28 and 29 for installation dates and summaries of interrogation information.

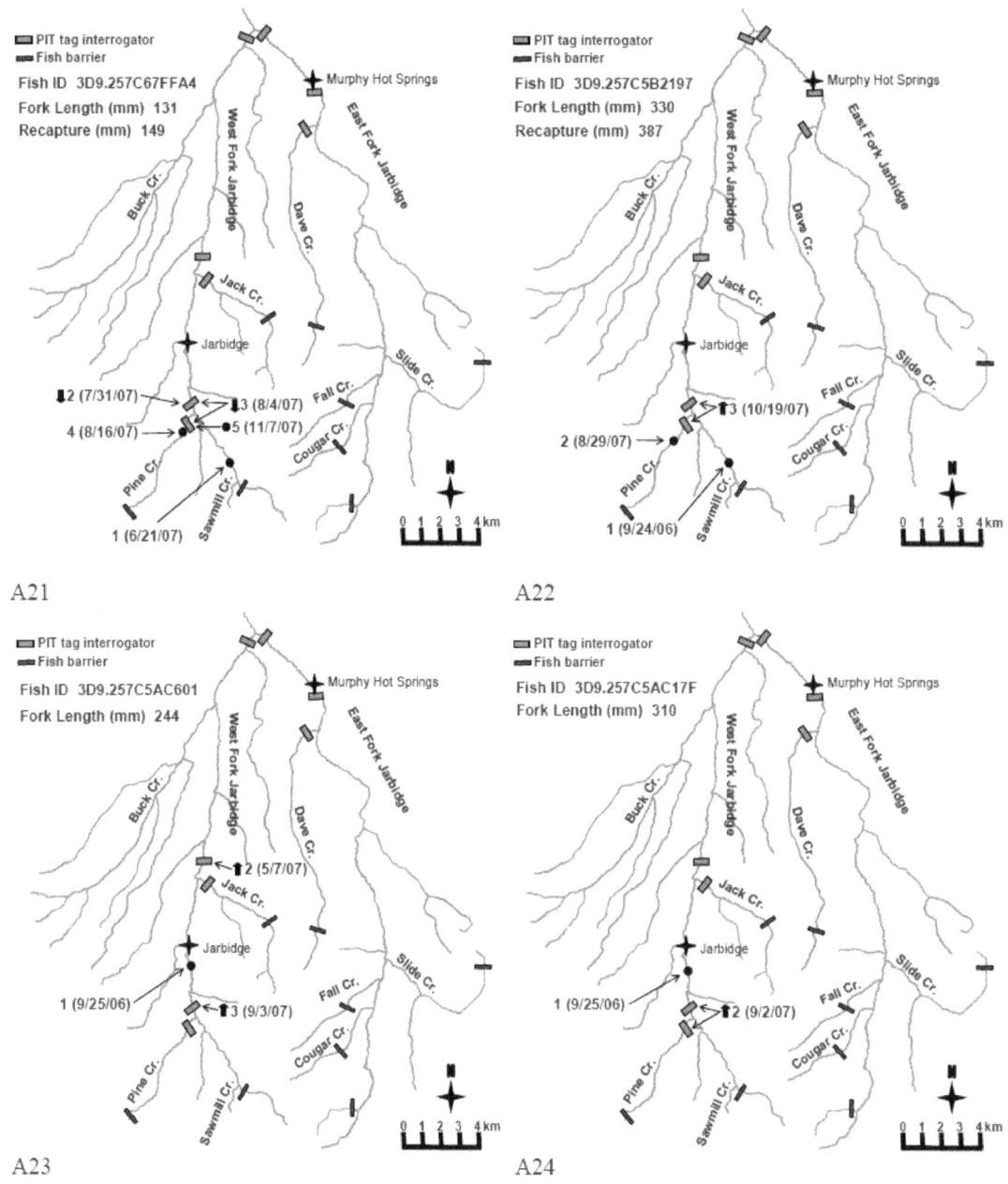

Figures A21 – A24. Movement of PIT-tagged bull trout within the Jarbidge River subbasin in 2006 and 2007. Each map represents a single bull trout and the number next to the symbol represents the order of events (1 = tagging, 2 = interrogation or recapture, 3 + = subsequent interrogation or recapture). See table 8 and figures 28 and 29 for installation dates and summaries of interrogation information.

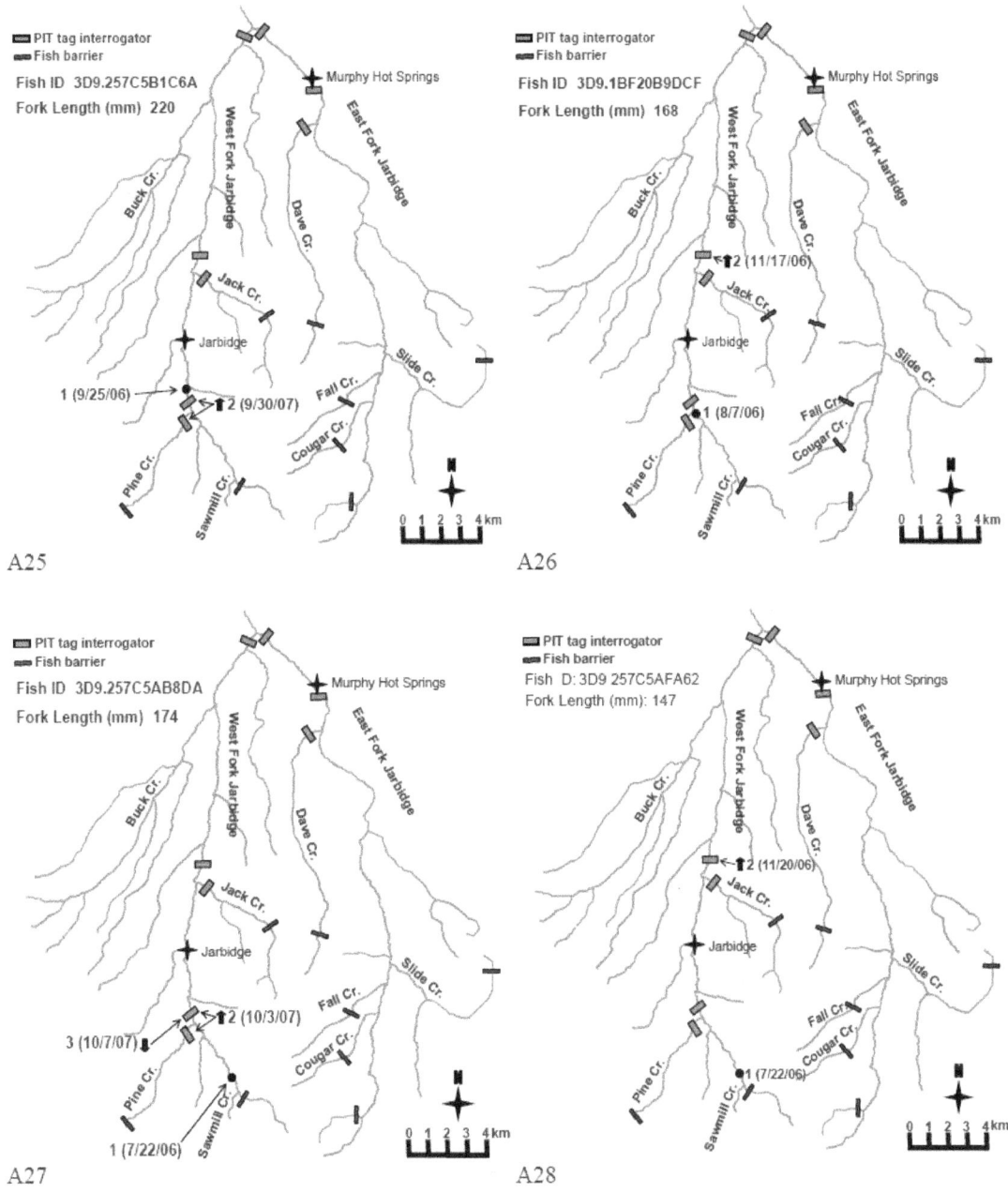

Figures A25 – A28. Movement of PIT-tagged bull within the Jarbidge River subbasin in 2006 and 2007. Each map represents a single bull trout and the number next to the symbol represents the order of events (1 = tagging, 2 = interrogation or recapture, 3 + = subsequent interrogation or recapture). See table 8 and figures 28 and 29 for installation dates and summaries of interrogation information.

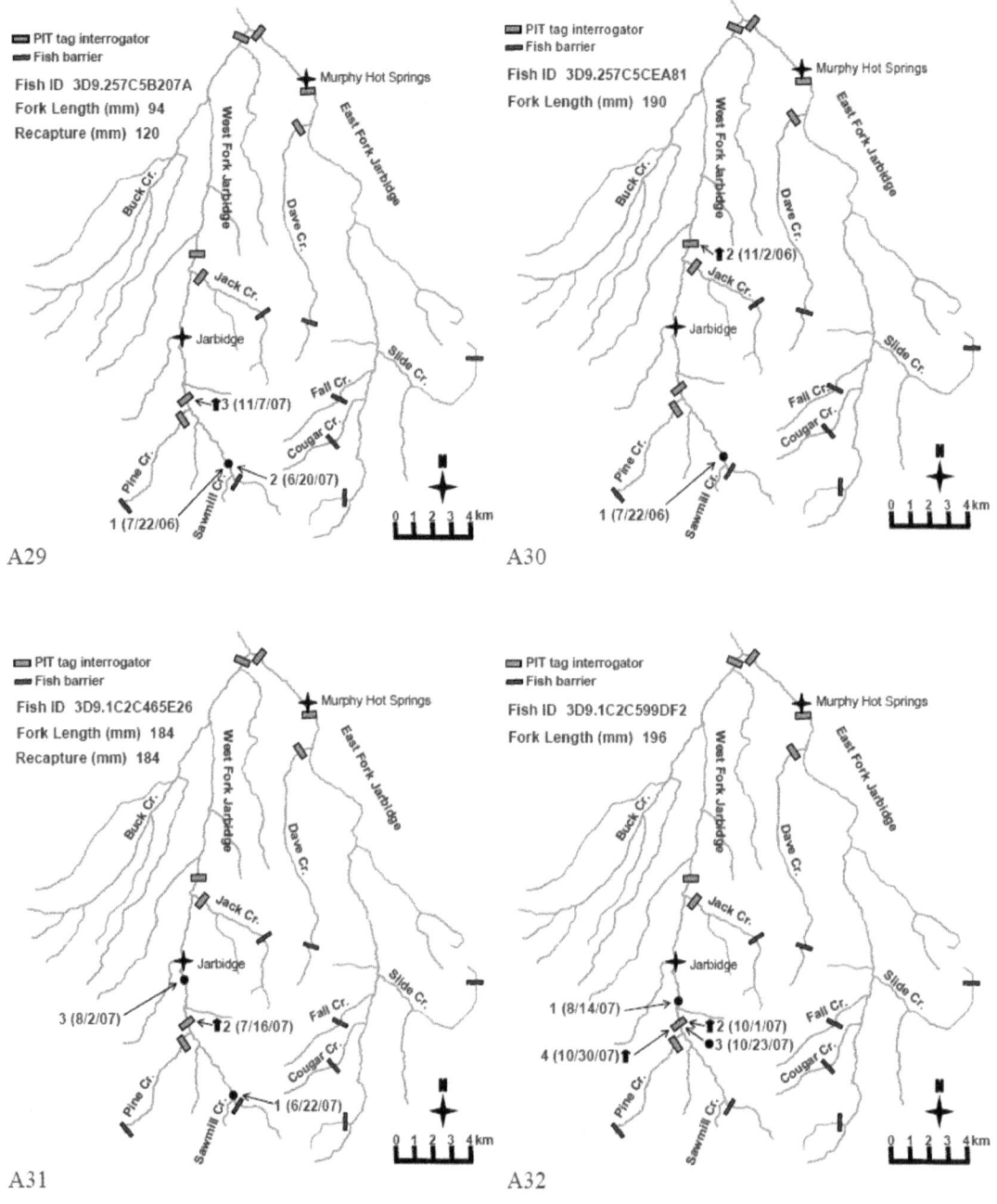

Figures A29 – A32. Movement of PIT-tagged bull trout within the Jarbidge River subbasin in 2006 and 2007. Each map represents a single bull trout and the number next to the symbol represents the order of events (1 = tagging, 2 = interrogation or recapture, 3 + = subsequent interrogation or recapture). See table 8 and figures 28 and 29 for installation dates and summaries of interrogation information.

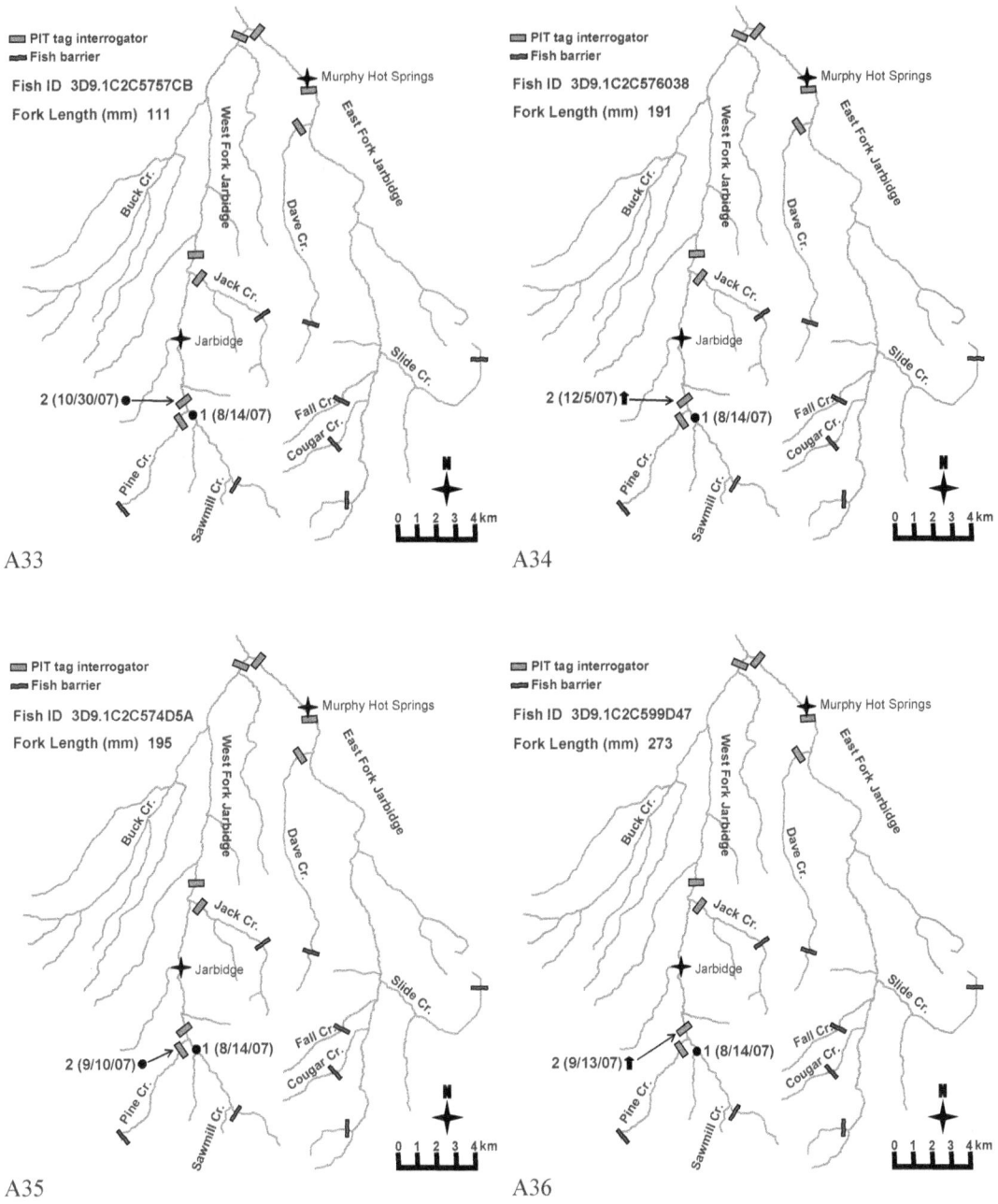

A33

A34

A35

A36

Figures A33 – A36. Movement of PIT-tagged bull trout within the Jarbidge River subbasin in 2006 and 2007. Each map represents a single bull trout and the number next to the symbol represents the order of events (1 = tagging, 2 = interrogation or recapture, 3 + = subsequent interrogation or recapture). See table 8 and figures 28 and 29 for installation dates and summaries of interrogation information.

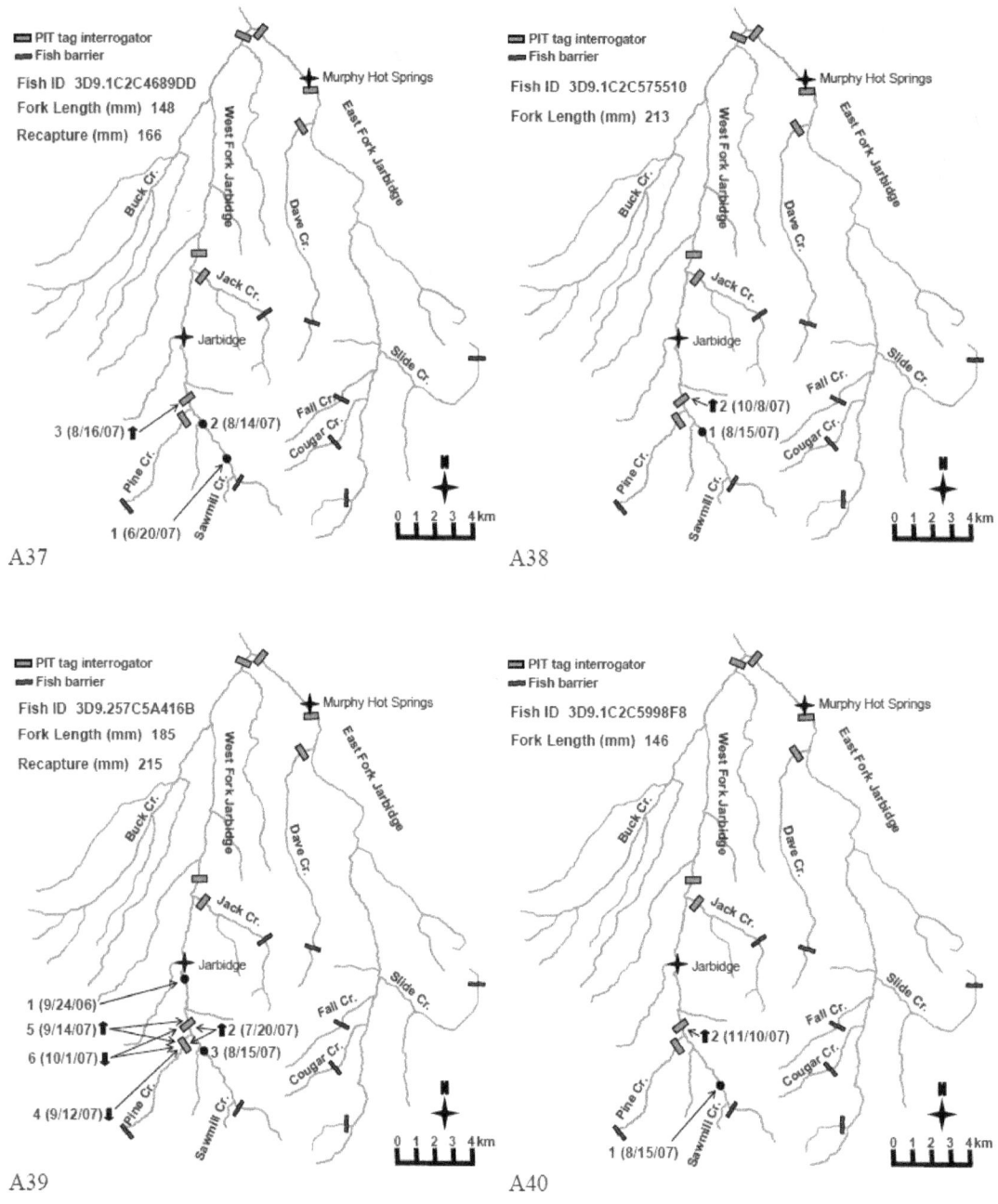

Figures A37 – A40. Movement of PIT-tagged bull trout within the Jarbidge River subbasin in 2006 and 2007. Each map represents a single bull trout and the number next to the symbol represents the order of events (1 = tagging, 2 = interrogation or recapture, 3 + = subsequent interrogation or recapture). See table 8 and figures 28 and 29 for installation dates and summaries of interrogation information.

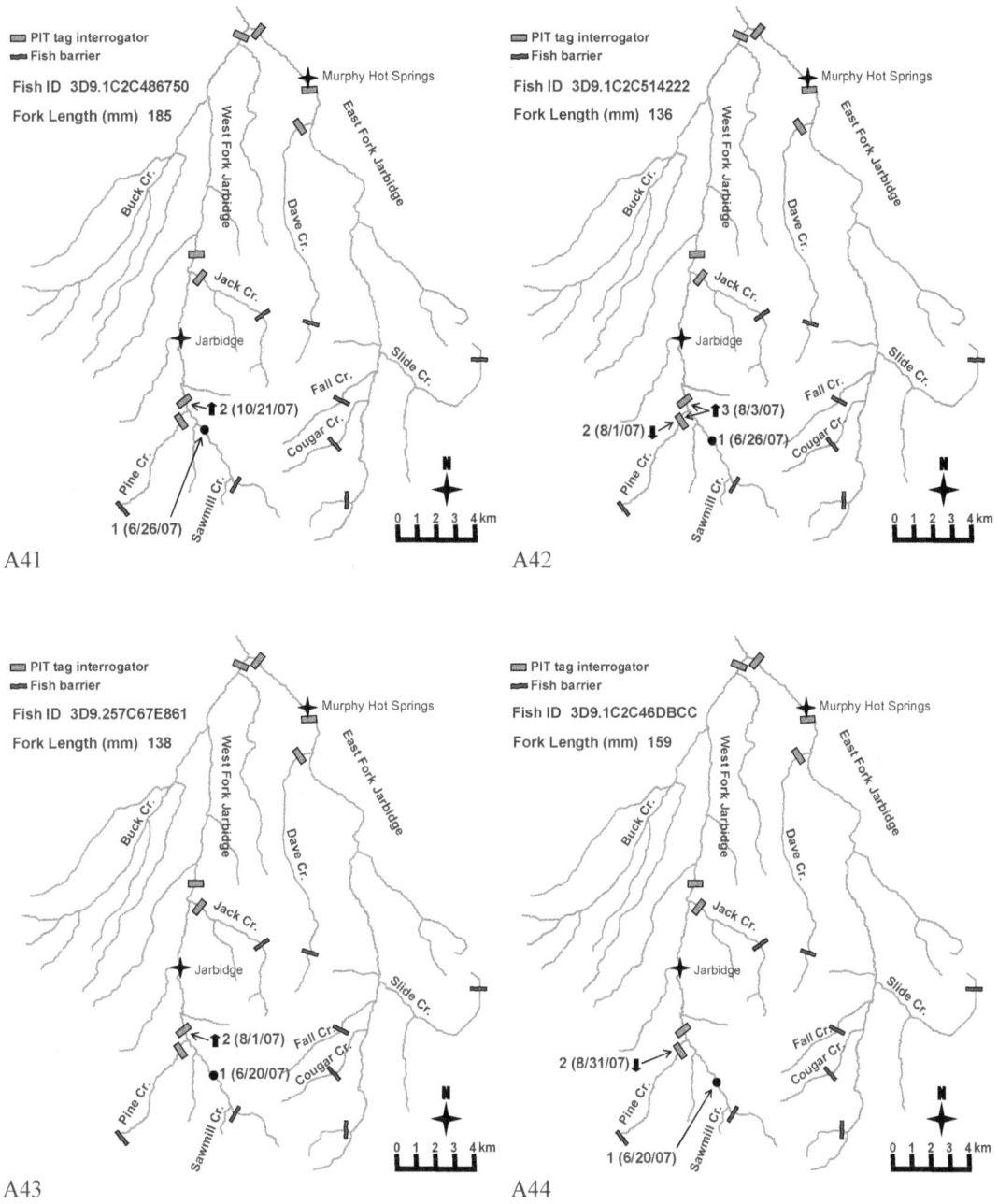

Figures A41 – A44. Movement of PIT-tagged bull trout within the Jarbidge River subbasin in 2006 and 2007. Each map represents a single bull trout and the number next to the symbol represents the order of events (1 = tagging, 2 = interrogation or recapture, 3 + = subsequent interrogation or recapture). See table 8 and figures 28 and 29 for installation dates and summaries of interrogation information.

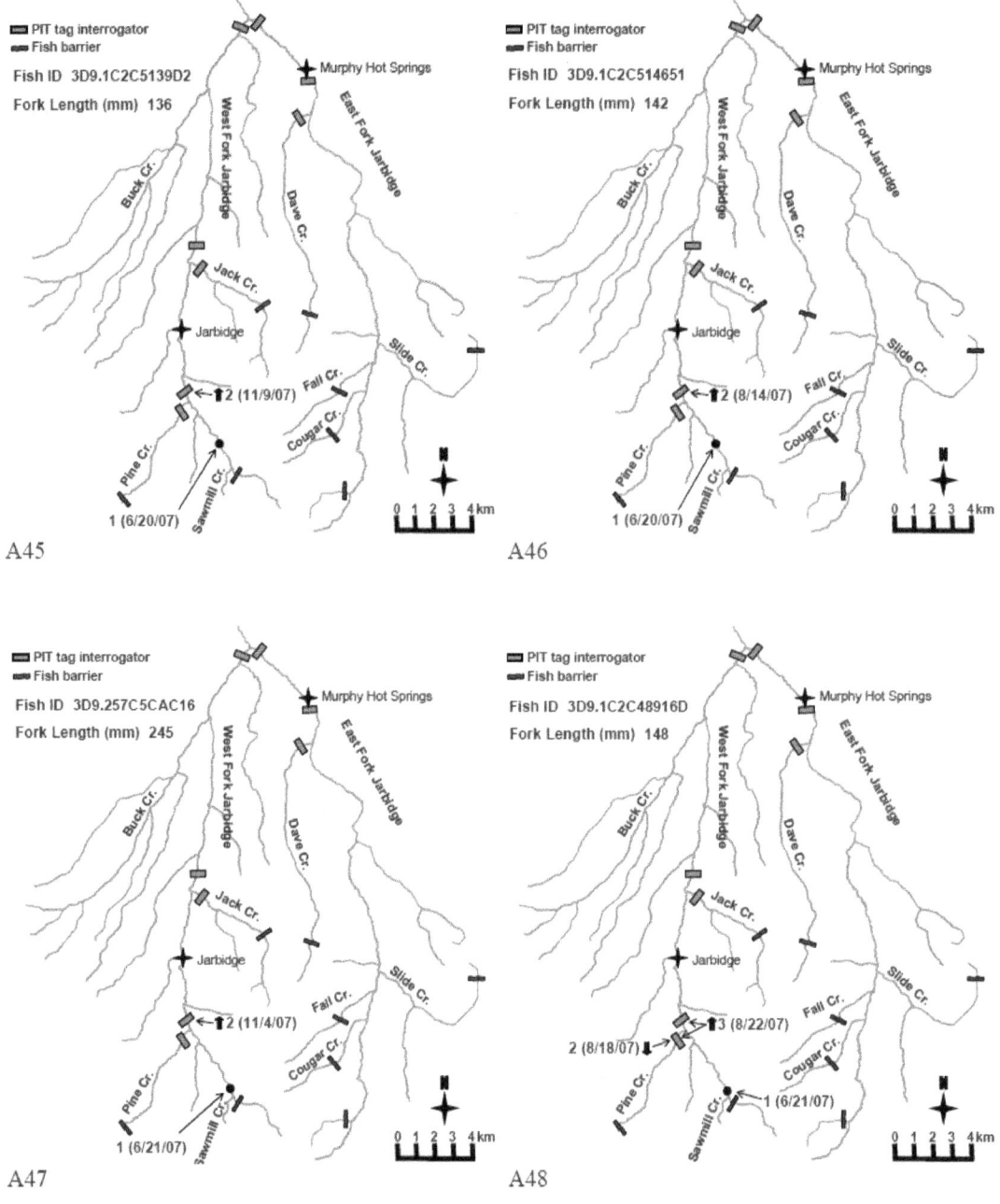

Figures A45 – A48. Movement of PIT-tagged bull trout within the Jarbidge River subbasin in 2006 and 2007. Each map represents a single bull trout and the number next to the symbol represents the order of events (1 = tagging, 2 = interrogation or recapture, 3 + = subsequent interrogation or recapture). See table 8 and figures 28 and 29 for installation dates and summaries of interrogation information.

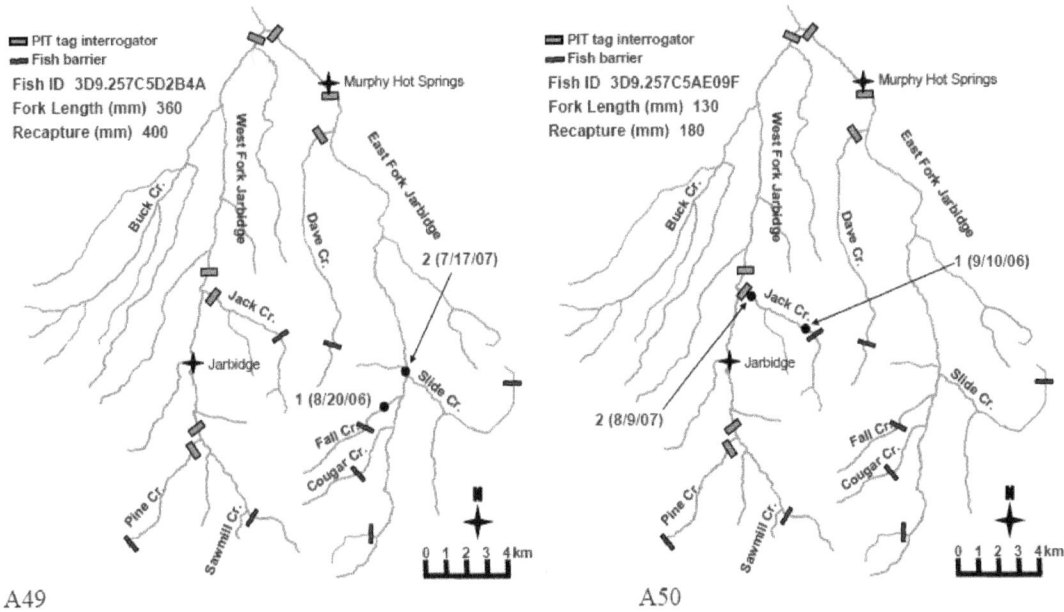

Figures A49 – A50. Movement of PIT-tagged bull trout that were within the Jarbidge River subbasin in 2006 and 2007. Each map represents a single bull trout and the number next to the symbol represents the order of events (1 = tagging, 2 = recapture).